MAM
HISTORY

Oakland Notes on the History
of Mayan-Mam Language

JAVIER ARMAS

Published by Javier's Organics

ISBN: 978-1-7362782-9-1

Mam History: Oakland Notes on the History of Mayan-Mam Language

Published May 20th, 2024. First Edition.

Published in Oakland, CA. USA.

Cover art by Sosa.

Oakland is home to one of the largest concentrations
of Mam speakers in the nation.[1]
- Los Angeles Times

Mayans started writing when English (even
Old English) had yet to be born.[2]
- Dennis Tedlock

Remember us after we have gone. Don't forget us. Conjure
up our faces and our words. Our image will be as dew
in the hearts of those who want to remember us.[3]
- *Popol Vuh*

---

[1] Cindy Carcamo, "Ancient Mayan languages are creating problems for today's immigration courts," Los Angeles Times. Aug. 9, 2016.

[2] Dennis Tedlock, *2000 Years of Mayan Literature*, 1.

[3] Rigoberta Menchú, *I, Rigoberta Menchú : An Indian Woman in Guatemala*, 188.

This book is dedicated to
the Mayan-Mam-speaking community
of students in Oakland.

CONTENTS

Introduction by Lorena Mendoza..xv

Introduction by Miguel Ortiz Martin xix

Twenty Words and Phrases in English and Mam by Lorena
and Miguel xxiii

Introduction by Javier Armas xxv

Chapter 1: "Sorry, I no speak English."....................................1

    A Short History of US' Linguistic Policies....................................... 3

    Language Extinction in the Era of Technology 7

Chapter 2: Ancient History of Mayan Language........................... 15

Chapter 3: Spanish Colonialism...35

Chapter 4: Independent Central America.................................... 49

Chapter 5: 20th Century Guatemala 57

Chapter 6: The Guatemalan Civil War.. 61

    Mayan Language Developments under Conditions of War 68

Chapter 7: Oakland...73

Chapter 8: Modern Linguistic Research......................................79

    General Interviews 90

        Miguel's Interviews... 94

        Lorena's Interviews 98

        Anjelica's Interviews..103

Chapter 9: Conclusion... 111

Bibliography... 115

Index.. 127

LIST OF FIGURES

1. Virgilio Aguilar Mendez, Mayan-Mam speaker, told Officer Kunovich, "Sorry, I no speak English." 1

2. Historical Bar Map of five major Languages: Proto-Mayan, Mam, Latin, English, and Spanish............ 6

3. Dendritic Tree Model of the Mayan language family............ 9

4. Mayan Temple 1, Tikal Guatemala 13

5. Mayan glyphs in the Palenque site museum, Palenque, Chiapas, Mexico............ 14

6. Linguistic Map showing Proto-Mayan in 2,200 BCE. 14

7. Map of Mayan Languages 1,500 BCE............ 16

8. Approximate migration routes and dates for various Mayan language families............ 16

9. Map of Mayan Languages from 750 BCE to 250 CE............ 18

10. Diversification of Western Mayan Languages............ 18

11. Diversification of Eastern Mayan Languages............ 19

12. Six pages of the Dresden Codex 20

13. Map of Eastern Mayan Languages. 21

14. Stone Stela, the Mayan writing system, was formed between 600 and 800 CE............ 22

15. Glyph blocks used for Mayan writing............ 23

16. Grid-like layout of glyphs that represent numbers............ 24

17. The Mayan numeral system is up from 0 to 19. 25

18. Chichén Itzá. 25

19. Tzolkin Mayan Calendar 260 day cycle. 27

20. Chichén Itzá during the day and up close. 28

21. Linguistic map of Mayan languages 1017 BCE 29

22. Linguistic map of Mayan languages 498 BCE. 29

23. Linguistic map of Mayan languages 3 AC 29

24. Linguistic map of Mayan languages 552 AC 30

25. Linguistic map of Mayan languages 1004 AC 30

26. Montezuma meets Cortés in 1519, Unknown artist. 33

27. Map of Mayan Languages in 1500 CE 34

28. Linguistic map of Mayan languages 1500 AC 35

29. Epidemic Map of Early Colonial Mexico, New Spain. 36

30. Linguistic map of Mayan languages in 1719 AC. 42

31. Yucatec Maya writing in the Dresden Codex, ca. 11–
    12th century, Chichen Itza 44

32. Central America's symbol was placed on the flag in 1821 47

33. Flag of Guatemala (1838-1843) 48

34. Map of Guatemala in 1829. 51

35. Map with stripes showing the decline of Mayan
    languages in 1881. 52

36. Flag of Guatemala in 1924. 52

37. "Gloriosa Victoria" by Diego Rivera 55

38. Pictured: Antonia Choc with her grandson.................................. 60

39. Map of Killings during the Civil War in Guatemala. 61

40. Map of Indigenous Populations in Guatemala.............................61

41. A sign in Guatemala that reads Wanted José Efraín
Ríos Montt for genocide in the 1980s.. 66

42. Immigration from Guatemala to the U.S. from 1990 to 2005 72

43. FIGURE 43: Logo for Radio B'ALAM Voces Maya....................74

44. Differing Mam dialects and their regions in Guatemala.............. 83

LIST OF LORENA'S AND MIGUEL'S BUBBLE THOUGHTS

1. Miguel reflects on the different Mayan languages. 11

2. Lorena reflects on Spanish colonialism. 39

3. Miguel reflects on the changing cultural customs
   moving away from their Mayan origin... 50

4. Lorena reflects on the origins of the Guatemalan civil war. 59

5. Lorena reflects on the ending of the Guatemalan civil war. 64

6. Lorena reflects on the declining use of Mam. 68

7. Lorena reflects on Mam media channels in the US 71

INTRODUCTION BY LORENA MENDOZA

My name is Lorena Mendoza. I was raised by parents who are of Guatemalan descent. My dad is from Todos Santos, Cuchumatan, and my mom is from Tzipoc, Aldea El Rancho, Guatemala. Both of these places are very beautiful; and although they are not far from each other, each has their own unique style. Before I was born, my parents decided to come to the U.S. My dad was the one who came to the U.S. first, and the story of my life began there.

My dad came because he was trying to find a convenient state for both of my parents to stay in, where they felt it was the right place to start a fresh chapter in their lives after they had left their country. During that time, my dad stayed in Saint Joseph, Missouri, for quite a while. This was where he finally found a stable job, could help my mom and begin their lives there. He decided to bring my mom with him after a year. After a short period of it just being the two of them, 2007 came – and that was the year I was born. When I was younger, my parents had a mix of languages in which they communicated with me, making me bilingual from an early age.

Since my dad was already getting more fluent in Spanish, he would talk to me in Spanish occasionally. On the other hand, my mom wasn't fluent in Spanish, so she would speak with me in Mam, our Mayan language. My parents always told me that "it's always good to learn the traditional language of where we come from because, in the future, it would be useful and give us good benefits in our careers or jobs." At the time, I didn't really put thought into it because where I was raised, it was mainly white people, and I rarely saw any Guatemalans. The only Guatemalans

I'd seen were my family members, who were the ones who lived beside us (since we lived at a duplex house), and this woman who used to take care of me and my little sister when my parents would go to work.

Besides them, I didn't see any Guatemalans, which is why I didn't really see the importance of learning Mam. Young me thought, who else would I communicate in Mam with besides my parents? But even after that, I still learned a few words in Mam. I would communicate with my family, even if I didn't speak it correctly since Mam has an accent and I couldn't pronounce certain words the way they should be said, I would still try my best. The way I learned how to pronounce words in Mam was from my dad. Since he went to school in Guatemala, he learned how to write in Mam, and because of that, it was useful for him to write down words in Mam and give them to me as homework to learn how to pronounce words. He first started helping me with the numbers in Mam because it was an easier way for him to start, and then, over time, we went on with words. Little did I know then the cultural significance of the words I was learning to speak.

I remember the first easy word I learned in Mam was the one for "tortilla", which is pronounced *wab'j*. Over time, I started practicing our Mayan language more and more, and I became fluent. I was finally comprehending what was being said in Mam between my family and the lady who looked after me.

I entered school at the age of 5; during this time I didn't know any English, so it was hard for me to communicate and understand what people were saying to me. Because of that I had a tutor come to my house every weekend to teach me English and because of that, it affected me in losing how to speak Mam. Because, like our neighbors, my school was mainly white people, there was only a little percentage of Latinos, and clearly where I was, it was only English speaking. I still didn't lose fluency in comprehension of what was being said in Mam; the only thing I lost over time was speaking it.

Years later, things changed again, when my parents decided to move us to Oakland. It was a big change for me because I had gotten used to where I was raised, and I didn't want to meet new people and go to a new school, especially because I was quiet and not really very well socialized. It really got to me, but the decision had been made.

So, in 2015, we came to Oakland because my parents had more family members there and had heard that Oakland had better financial opportunities for families. When we arrived in Oakland, I was really shocked by the fact that there were a lot of Mayan people that included me. It was so different because I came from a very distinctive place, and comparing this to my previous school was really surprising to me. When I was accepted into a new school, I saw a good amount of Guatemalans. I felt like I actually belonged somewhere where I could relate to other people, like their traditions, and their clothing. What made me happier was that they actually would speak Mam, too.

Even though I lost the capacity to speak it, I did get certain words right when we spoke it for fun. When I got older, I saw that many people from other races, like white people, Arabs, Asians, and others had a desire to learn our Mayan language. It was certainly a change from the life I had lived growing up.

To any newcomers to the United States, I want them to know that they should never be ashamed of their cultural identity. Coming from a unique country and knowing that people from other races visit as tourists to learn about Guatemala's background, it was an honor for our country to receive such recognition. I say recognition because I rarely hear stories/history about Guatemala, such as its wars, traditions, etc. But we, as Mayans, should be able to keep the culture alive and never forget our dialect because it is such a benefit being able to speak and know three languages, which can bring us a brighter future.

Overall, from the research, I have learned much about Mayan history that I did not know before, such as the distinct languages that exist in Guatemala and the formation of the culture.

From my perspective, I know that my relationship with Mam remains the same because it's something that will keep being communicated in my family so that the next generation keeps up with their culture and represents it in its authentic, beautiful way.

Lastly, the interviews I did regarding the Mayan language were great. I got to learn from other Mayans what they knew about the Mayan language. This has allowed me to understand more about the formation of Mam, and this will help other people who are also Mayan-related to learn more about their culture and keep passing it on to new generations that will get to learn about Guatemalan history.

HIGHLIGHT

When we arrived in Oakland, I was really shocked by the fact that there were a lot of Mayan people that included me. It was so different because I came from a very distinctive place, and comparing this to my previous school was really surprising to me. When I was accepted into a new school, I saw a good amount of Guatemalans. I felt like I actually belonged somewhere where I could relate to other people, like their traditions, and their clothing. What made me happier was that they actually would speak Mam, too.

1. What impact does Mayan and Guatemalan people of Oakland have on Lorena's experience?

INTRODUCTION BY MIGUEL ORTIZ MARTIN

My name is Miguel. I was born and raised in Guatemala for eight years before migrating to the U.S. During the years I was in Guatemala, I was raised by my grandparents, uncles, aunts, and cousins. My mom was in my life. She just had to move to the U.S. way earlier than I did in the hope of giving me a better life. Growing up wasn't easy, but it wasn't as hard knowing that I was surrounded by family. I had caring family members, as well as most of my necessities.

During my childhood, I learned to speak Mam, which, at the time, was our only form of communication. Thanks to relatives and friends who spoke it on a daily basis, I became fluent. When I was around six years old, Spanish became known in the town where I lived, although it wasn't actually called Spanish. Back then and to this day, we call it 'Castellano,' which is a little different from regular Spanish. Castellano began to be implemented in local schools, and then it became the language used for learning in my local school.

Being me, I didn't learn a single thing, nor did I want to. I thought that it was enough that I could already communicate with my family and friends, and I believed everyone outside my town spoke Mam. Every now and then, my grandparents would go to nearby cities for our necessities. During those trips, I began to understand that Mam wasn't a common language, and I started to notice this weird language barrier. To my mind, I knew only those who looked and dressed similarly to me would be able to speak Mam. Around seven years old, I was told to learn *Castellano*, and so I tried to little avail.

Not so long after, I was sent to the U.S. and having learned nothing except to speak Mam, it became a problem. I started attending elementary school in California, where I could not communicate with teachers or students. This led me to be the kid who sat alone and did nothing the entire day. Every week, kids and teachers talked and talked, but all I could do was stare blankly at them. This went on for a few months before my mom decided it would be best to come home earlier from work each night and study one-on-one with me. She, in fact, did not go easy on me. I vividly remember times when she would be harsh and angry if I didn't learn at a fast enough pace. But thanks to that, I was able to learn Spanish at a quick rate, along with the small amount of English she knew.

From then on, I took charge, and school became a little easier for me. Finally, I was able to speak with classmates, although not at the same level as them, but to the point they could understand me. After 4th grade, the language barrier holding me back was officially gone. I had learned two new languages and became fluent in them, all that while also retaining my first ever language, making me able to say that I'm trilingual, although I wasn't taught to write in Mam.

During middle school, I remember being a bystander to a young boy getting bullied by students who knew no better. It turned out that the reason he was getting bullied was because of his ethnicity. He was Guatemalan, but that wasn't the problem. The problem started when that same boy started to change how he was. I noticed from afar that he wanted to change his identity just to fit in, scared to represent his real identity.

Fast forward, It wasn't until years later that I was able to travel back to Guatemala and noticed major changes. Some of them were noticeable. For example, my hometown was a lot bigger, cities looked bigger, and plazas were filled with all types of things. Shockingly, more and more Mayans or Mayan descendants also became modern – leaving the Mayan traditions behind.

Little by little, I fear that the Mayan culture and language will be at risk of becoming extinct. That is why, educating people about the Mayan

Mam and its culture is important to reopen minds and keep it alive. It also prevents its people from being ashamed of their roots, especially the newer generations to come.

In doing this research, I have gained a lot more knowledge about the Mayan Mam history in general, including when Mam was formed and how many languages were formed from a single root. My relationship with Mam remains the same, and I'll still use it as my primary communication form with my family. From my interviews, it has become clear that this book will pass on important, missing or forgotten knowledge to people, including those from Guatemala who have forgotten or never learned its history.

HIGHLIGHT

From then on, I took charge, and school became a little easier for me. Finally, I was able to speak with classmates, although not at the same level as them, but to the point they could understand me. After 4th grade, the language barrier holding me back was officially gone. I had learned two new languages and became fluent in them, all that while also retaining my first ever language, making me able to say that I'm trilingual, although I wasn't taught to write in Mam.

1. How did learning two new languages help form Miguel's confidence for learning?

TWENTY WORDS AND PHRASES IN ENGLISH AND MAM BY LORENA AND MIGUEL

1) Sour taste - Tx'om

2) Blood - Chi'y

3) Eat - Wál

4) Wash - Txjol

5) Buy- Laq'ol

6) To learn - Xnaq'tzal

7) House - Já

8) Rest - Ajlal

9) Tomorrow- Nchi'j

10) Dog -Tx'yan

11) Mother - k'txu

12) Father- kx'man

13) Grandmother - Ná

14) Grandfather - Tat

15) Baby - shla'jx

16) People - xj'al

17) Cat - Wish

18) Arm- kx'ab

19) Stomach- n'guj

20) Let's go to sleep- xco' wah'tal

INTRODUCTION BY JAVIER ARMAS

"Mayan mathematics go back thousands of years, utilizing 20, not 10, as the basis for their numerical system," as I explain across a sea of Skyline high school students in the Oakland hills. The student body was incredibly diverse, with an array of different cultures mixed well together, a hallmark of Oakland's landscape. A significant number of such students are recent migrants from Guatemala. Out of this Guatemalan migratory group, many, roughly half speak Mam, a Mayan language. I lived in Mexico City studying Mayan mathematics, preparing to create a history of Mayan mathematics. As I taught this unit a Skyline I met an array of Mayan Mam speaking Guatemalan born students in my classes, many of these students were electrified by the unit on Mayan mathematics, and myself by simply connecting and teaching Mayan mathematics to teeanger Mayans in Oakland. They articulated a connection to my Mayan mathematics unit, as they told their parents. Many students told me I had been the first official American teacher to teach them on Mayan content. It is usually a private matter from their parents and close knit community. I told myself I must pause my history of Mayan mathematics to better understand why there are so many Mam speaking Mayan migrants in Oakland. My students became my guides and the academic work was the content we sifted through.

As a historian I thought what histories of Mam are there? Not much. There was grammar of Mam and histories of Guatemala, but no history of Mam. From that point, I started my mission to help generate a historical understanding for the Mayan-Mam language utilizing both academic, linguistic, historical works already written and fresh interviews with Mam native speakers asking what they know about the history of Mam. If, on the one hand, we can summarize the important historical points from academic work already published, like what Howard Zinn did in his *A People's History of the United States*, and add insights from new interviews with Mam native speakers on their historical memory, we could then mix, or synthesize, the academic writings with fresh interviews to both *generate* and *preserve* Mam history. This carries an important meaning as Mam is considered a severely endangered language.[4] We were proud that this history we worked on of the Mam language could hopefully contribute to preserving Mam as a language as it faces a threat of extinction.

Our research consisted of thirty academic history, linguistic, sociology and anthropology books, thirty academic articles, eighteen media articles, eleven academic exhibitions, and eight government documents. We also conducted over twenty-five interviews of native Mam speakers composed to understand their historical memory of Mam as a language. This book aspires to put all our findings together to help students make sense of the history of the Mam language.

Lorena was in my 11th grade US History and Miguel in my 12th grade Government/Economics class. We meet once to twice a week, researching articles, doing and reviewing interviews, and developing this book. Lorena, Miguel and Anjelica all conducted interviews, in Mam and Spanish, that you will find at the end of the book. Anjelica had to leave for personal reasons. She exhibited remarkable trilingual skills, interviewing in Mam and writing in English and still utilizing Spanish. Miguel did interviews in Mam, commanding greater usage of the language. Lorena interviewed in Spanish, as she is developing her Mam, even though Mam is deeply built into her linguistic foundation.

This book also inspires me to help develop a movement of histories of indigenous languages. For example, my father is from El Salvador

---

[4] Moseley, Christopher, ed. "Atlas of the World's Languages in Danger." 2010.

which is home to the Nahua (often problematically referred to as Pipil) who speak Nawat, a Nahuan language, part of the Uto-Aztecan language family.[5] No history of the Nawat language exists in the English language. Compared to European languages, robust histories of English, Spanish, French, Latin and Greek languages permeate libraries around the world. This book taught me how powerful it is to both study and create the history of a language.

When we wrote this book, we wanted to create a textbook to help high school students understand their own history, as Guatemalan Mam students rapidly increase enrollment at Rudsdale, Fremont, Castlemont, Skyline, Oakland High, Oakland International, McClymonds, Coliseum College Preparatory Academy and Oakland Tech high schools. We also wanted to serve incoming college students and working adults who attend Laney, Merritt, Alameda and Berkeley City College. At the time of writing this book I was teaching 11th grade US History, 12th grade Government/ Economics at Skyline High School, and Introduction to US History at Laney College. I myself spoke Spanish as my first language, was born and raised in Oakland and had a horrible experience only speaking Spanish when I started schooling in the Oakland public schools. The challenges built within language and territory are real. This project resonated with a difficult part of my own complex linguistic history.

There was limited time to create the book's first edition, as we sought to produce physical copies by May 20th 2024, for the end of the 2023-2024 school year. We also envision the ability to build off this book with more developed editions in the coming years. My hope is Lorena, Miguel and others alike grab the torch of the historian, and write new robust and insightful histories of Mam that have yet to exist. The framework of this book was inspired by our home, Oakland, which has always had a soul of resilience and politics of resistance; a friendly landscape for the growing Mam community.

---

[5] Campbell, Lyle. *The Pipil Language of El Salvador / Lyle Campbell.* Berlin ; Mouton Publishers, 1985.

HIGHLIGHT

As a historian I thought what histories of Mam are there? Not much. There was grammar of Mam and histories of Guatemala, but no history of Mam. From that point, I started my mission to help generate a historical understanding for the Mayan-Mam language utilizing both academic, linguistic, historical works already written and fresh interviews with Mam native speakers asking what they know about the history of Mam. If, on the one hand, we can summarize the important historical points from academic work already published…and add insights from new interviews with Mam native speakers on their historical memory, we could then mix, or synthesize, the academic writings with fresh interviews to both *generate* and *preserve* Mam history.

1. How does combining academic research with interviews from native Mam speakers contribute to understanding and preserving the historical narrative of the Mam language and culture?

"SORRY, I NO SPEAK ENGLISH."

FIGURE 1 Virgilio Aguilar Mendez, Mayan-Mam speaker, told Officer Kunovich, "Sorry, I no speak English."

On May 19, 2023, a 19-year-old immigrant Guatemalan Mayan-Mam speaker named Virgilio Aguilar Mendez was apprehended by Florida police. Outside of Motel 8. Officer Kunovich attempts to apprehend Mendez, while Mendez responds, "Sorry, I no speak English."[6] A tussle en-

---

[6] S. Helling, S and S. Algar (2024, March 2). Charges dropped against migrant accused in the death of Florida deputy who had heart attack after struggle. *New York Post*. https://nypost.com/2024/03/01/us-news/charges-dropped-against-migrant-accused-in-the-death-of-florida-deputy-who-had-heart-attack-after-struggle/

sued, and Officer Kunovich shortly suffered a heart attack, collapsed, and later died. Mendez was then charged with felony murder of a Florida police officer.[7] The autopsy report concluded Kunovich died of natural causes after suffering cardiac dysrhythmia, an irregular heartbeat.[8] Mendez was in jail for over six months, waiting for his trial. A petition circulated arguing that Mendez's fourth constitutional right "against unreasonable searches and seizures" was violated and garnered more than six hundred thousand signatures from January 3 to February of 2024.[9] On March 1, 2024, the charges were dropped. The District State Attorney's office acknowledges that the language barrier was a factor in the case, commenting on the problem of "the defendant's inability to comprehend the English language."[10]

Mendez did not speak English or Spanish. He spoke Mam, one of the thirty-two Mayan languages with ancient historical roots. The Mayan-Mam community has suffered horrible attacks throughout history, from Spanish colonialism to the recent civil war ending in 1996 – and despite laws, the challenges continue. Leaders from the Mam community have emerged to promote the linguistic revitalization of the Mam language. This book aspires to contextualize the history of the Mam language. It combines key research from historians, anthropologists, and linguistics on Mam into a historical framework. Such a historical framework is combined with Mam-speaking high school students interviewing native Mam speakers about their understanding of Mam, including what they know about the history of Mam.

The Mam is a Mayan indigenous group of around 500,000 residing

---

[7] D. Merchan (2024, January 10). *Petition calls for release of Guatemalan teen charged with officer's death following heart attack.* ABC News. https://abcnews.go.com/US/petition-calls-release-guatemalan-teen-charged-officers-death/story?id=106225689

[8] C. Barbeito (2024, January 3). *Farmworker charged in officer's heart failure death during arrest.* Mitú. https://wearemitu.com/wearemitu/news/guatemalan-farmworker-charged-death-police/

[9] "Sign the Petition." *Change.org*, https://www.change.org/p/release-virgilio-aguilar-mendez-immediately. Accessed 18 Jan. 2024.

[10] S. Helling and S. Algar (2024, March 2). Charges dropped against migrant accused in the death of Florida deputy who had heart attack after struggle. *New York Post.* https://nypost.com/2024/03/01/us-news/charges-dropped-against-migrant-accused-in-the-death-of-florida-deputy-who-had-heart-attack-after-struggle/

in Guatemala's Western Highlands, southwestern coastal Guatemala, and parts of the state of Chiapas in Mexico. Mam populations are found in Guatemala's Huehuetenango, San Marcos, and western Quetzaltenango departments.[11] Mam communities have been forming in and around Los Angeles, Chicago, West Palm Beach, and, most recently, Oakland and California. Crecencio Ramirez, founder of Mam radio platform Radio B'ALAM in Oakland, remarks that the 2020 census recorded 20,000 Mam-speaking Guatemalans in Oakland. However, he notes that children were not counted and claimed the population of Mam speakers is really closer to 30,000 to 40,000.[12] Such numbers suggest that Oakland could be home to more than five percent of the total Mam population. In 2019, 2,500 Guatemalan migrants were detained along the U.S.-Mexico border– half of them were Mayan, and most spoke little or no Spanish at all.[13] Oakland Oakland Unified School District in 2023 reports that 1,130 students in their district speak Mam at home.[14]

A SHORT HISTORY OF US' LINGUISTIC POLICIES

The history of the U.S. has been shown to utilize English as the central, hegemonic, ruling language. However, Congress has never actually made English the official language of the United States, which is a distinguishing factor in American law.[15] The United States does administer English

[11] Wesley M. Collins, *The Heart of the Matter: Seeking the Center in Maya-Mam Language and Culture*, 46.

[12] Jose Martinez, CBS News. (2023, Sept.27) "Community in Oakland's Fruitvale District works to save ancient Guatemalan language."

[13] Ayala Jesus, "Oakland's Mayan Diaspora Overcomes Language Barriers and Finds Refuge in Radio B'alam" 150-151.

[14] Language revitalization in Oakland: A visual interview with Tessa Scott. (2023, August 21). Social Science Matrix.

[15] Marc Shell, *Wampum and the Origins of American Money*, 12.

as the dominant language and has done so by force, with roots in English colonialism. The first enslaved Africans in the U.S. area were in English colonial Virginia in the early 1600s, who initially spoke Niger-Congo-related African languages which were brutally suppressed by violence. African languages were lost in the U.S., but many sayings and cultural practices continue, such as the usage of *Mmhmmm* as a sound that represents thinking.[16] After the formation of the United States, slavery was legally intact in the South, with cotton agriculture expanding as an industry. Illiteracy was law, and it was illegal to teach enslaved Africans how to read and write in the United States, with punishments of 10 days in jail and being whipped with 39 lashes.[17] The diversity of languages in this English dominant environment. English writer Henry James points out that the immigrant communities in New York created the largest linguistic diversity in the world.[18]

The 1800s witnessed Native American boarding schools forming and applying an English-only policy, generationally eliminating native languages.[19] Administered by the U.S. military, the usage of English as the official language in present-day California and the Southwest was a result of the Mexican-American war. The U.S. conquest of Northern Mexico in 1848 was quicker; integrating 100,000 Spanish-speaking Mexican and indigenous people in the U.S. Hawaii's linguistic change was a bit slower. In 1831, pro-United States political operators and Christian missionaries published English textbooks and formed Christian schools on the Hawaiian islands. In the 1800s, the Native Hawaiian Kanaka teachers declined in influence, and by 1893, the oppressive school system, under pro-US Christian directors, mandated English as the only offi-

---

[16] Kumari Devarajan, "Ready for A Linguistic Controversy? Say 'Mmhmm.'" *NPR*, NPR, 17 Aug. 2018, https://www.npr.org/sections/codeswitch/2018/08/17/606002607/ready-for-a-linguistic-controversy-say-mhmm.

[17] William Goodell, *The American Slave Code in Theory and Practice*, 321.

[18] Marc Shell, *Wampum and the Origins of American Money*, 11.

[19] Richard Henry Pratt, *Battlefield and Classroom : Four Decades with the American Indian, 1867-1904.*, xxi.

cial language.[20] By 1896, the language Laws of the Republic of Hawaii were in full effect; "The English Language shall be the medium and basis of instruction in all public and private schools."[21] In 1907, U.S. President Theodore Roosevelt launched the English-only movement, which is still recognized today. In 1918, during World War I, Iowa Gov. William Harding passed the Babel Proclamation, banning the use of all non-English languages in schools, trains, meetings, churches, and even on the phone.[22] During World War II, the U.S. Government prohibited the use of the Japanese language amongst Japanese-Americans in the "Assembly Camps."[23] In 1967, Governor of California Ronald Reagan, facing a powerful social movement for civil and educational rights, signed Senate Bill 53, which ended a 95-year span that required all schools to offer instruction in English. The following year, President Johnson signed Title VII of the Elementary and Secondary Education Act, providing funds, staff, and materials for limited English learners.[24] In 1998, proposition 227 eliminated bilingual education in California's public schools, reinforcing English only in the most linguistically diverse state in the country. The policies of English dominating as a language flow through the country's history, from the founding of English pilgrims to the current political news.

In 2000, President Clinton signed Executive Order 13166, which requires federal agencies to assist people with limited English proficiency. Linguist Megan Simon reports, "[there are a number of challenges in implementing

[20] David Chang, *The World and All the Things upon It: Native Hawaiian Geographies of Exploration*, 227-228.

[21] Congress, United States. (1898). *Congressional Edition*. U.S. Government Printing Office, 1–PA23.

[22] Dennis Baron, "The Babel Proclamation: Celebrating a Century of Banning Foreign Languages in America." *Illinois.edu*, https://blogs.illinois.edu/view/25/653544. Accessed 21 Jan. 2024.

[23] Takeya Mizuno, "Government Suppression of the Japanese Language in World War II Assembly Camps." *Journalism & mass communication quarterly* 80.4 (2003), 849–865.

[24] *Stanford Education*, https://web.stanford.edu/~hakuta/www/policy/ELL/timeline.html. Accessed 15 Feb. 2024.

Executive Order 13166, in particular regarding fair access for speakers of indigenous languages." Simon also points to the US Census Bureau detailing 380 languages, "but does not not distinguish between individual languages in the Mayan family" let alone different dialects of Mam.[25]

Years Old

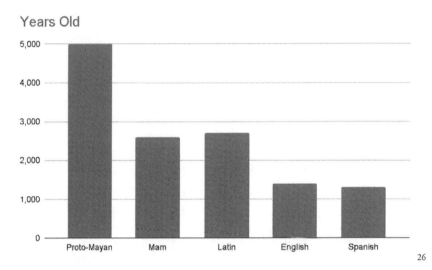

[26]

FIGURE 2 Historical Bar Map of five major Languages: Proto-Mayan, Mam, Latin, English, and Spanish.

---

[25] Simon, Megan, "A Phonetic Distance Approach to Intelligibility between Mam Regional Dialects." 1.

[26] Proto-Mayan broke up with the formation of 30+ Mayan languages, including Mam, just as Latin birthed approximately 47 Latin-related languages.

LANGUAGE EXTINCTION IN THE ERA OF TECHNOLOGY

The historical backdrop of the English-centered state policy has been met with the rapid growth of technology and AI. The modern wave of technological growth armed with artificial intelligence creates an ever heavier data environment, once again threatening older traditional cultures that could be seen as old and useless. The culture of a fast-paced environment, backed by advancements in technology, pose massive threats to anything that may be considered outdated – despite being culturally significant. Unfortunately, this reality encompasses indigenous languages all across the world, emphasizing the need for proper documentation with the goal of preservation.[27]

Mayan languages date back five thousand years to a singular proto-Mayan language. With the arrival of the Spanish, Mayan languages have been consistently under attack for the last five hundred years. As soon as the Spanish Catholics stepped foot in the Americas, all the way up to modern state-sponsored violence in the 1980s, Mayans have often been met with the threat of death for refusing to use a secondary tongue, with the incomers seeing it as opposing cultural assimilation. Such hostility did not alter the fact that the Proto-Mayan writing system is considered one of the most sophisticated writing systems in pre-modern times.[28] The Proto-Mayan language is split into more than thirty languages.[29] The Mayan language known as K'iche is the largest spoken of the Mayan languages, with about 1,000,000 speakers, and then Mam is second. Mayan language scholars, Mateo G.R. 'Nim B'ajlom' and Sandra Chigüela write, "Although Mayan Languages are

---

[27] Lenore A. Grenoble, Lenore and Lindsay J. Whaley, *Endangered Languages: Language Loss and Community Response* Frontmatter, *vii*.

[28] Shantal Garces, "The Origins of the Mayan Language and How It's Survived to Today." *Babbel Magazine*, Babbel, 12 June 2023, https://www.babbel.com/en/magazine/mayan-language.

[29] Miguel commented that he asked friends and relatives if they knew around how many mayan languages and they think there were, at most around 5 different languages.

one of the most well-documented groups of Amerindian Languages from Mesoamerica, they still remain quite a bleak and obscure topic."[30]

Within this context, it is interesting to see the community of Guatemalan Mayan-Mam speakers develop in Oakland, California, becoming the biggest newcomer group.[31] Oakland schools reported Guatemala surpassed Mexico as the top country of origin for new students, bringing Mam-speaking youth to the classrooms.[32]

According to the U.S. Department of Justice, Mam recently joined existing research, putting it among the top 10 languages used during court hearings.[33] Despite this, linguists explain the realities of indigenous languages dying. Linguists Whaley and Lenore explain a "number of languages which will simply cease to be spoken in the next fifty to a hundred years," referring to this as "[the] phenomenon of language death," which is heavily prevalent in indigenous communities.[34] To further explain how serious the threat of dying indigenous languages is, Linguist Clifton Pye asserts that there is only acquisition data, how one learns a language, for only 3% of the world's 6,000 plus languages.[35] In 2016, the United Nations General Assembly demonstrated concerns that 40% of the world's estimated 6,700 languages were in danger of dying, with Pye

[30] Mateo G.R. 'Nim B'ajlom' and Sandra Chigüela. *A comparison of four Mayan languages: From Mexico to Guatemala*, 7

[31] Romero, F. J. (n.d.). *Do you speak Mam? Growth of Oakland's Guatemalan community sparks interest in indigenous language*. KQED. Retrieved December 27, 2023, from https://www.kqed.org/news/11763374/do-you-speak-mam-growth-of-oaklands-guatemalan-community-sparks-interest-in-indigenous-language

[32] F. J. Romero (n.d.). *Do you speak Mam? Growth of Oakland's Guatemalan community sparks interest in indigenous language*. KQED. Retrieved December 27, 2023, from https://www.kqed.org/news/11763374/do-you-speak-mam-growth-of-oaklands-guatemalan-community-sparks-interest-in-indigenous-language

[33] *U.S. department OF JUSTICE EXECUTIVE OFFICE FOR IMMIGRATION REVIEW STATISTICS YEARBOOK FY DOJ executive office for immigration review (EOIR)*. (2017). Justice.gov. https://www.justice.gov/eoir/page/file/1107056/download

[34] Lenore A. Grenoble, Lenore and Lindsay J. Whaley. "Endangered Languages: Language Loss and Community Response Frontmatter, *vii*.

[35] Clifton Pye, "Documenting the acquisition of indigenous languages." 454.

pointing out, "the majority belonging to indigenous peoples."[36] [37] That same year, the United Nations General Assembly passed a resolution (A/RES/71/178) proclaiming 2019 as the International Year of Indigenous Languages. As mentioned, Mam is considered a severely endangered language.[38]

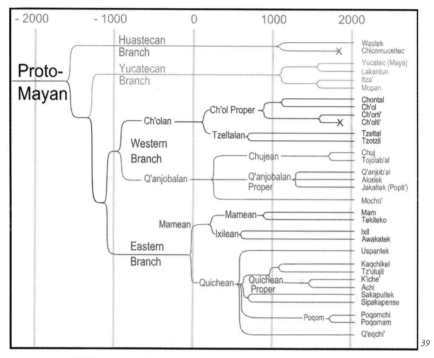

FIGURE 3 Dendritic Tree Model of the Mayan language family.

The linguistic diversity of the Americas is also very rich, ranging from

[36] Ibid..

[37] Miguel writes, "This is because most colonizers tried getting rid of native languages, because according to my previous knowledge they feared they communicated plans to fight back. also because of religious beliefs."

[38] Moseley, Christopher, ed. "Atlas of the World's Languages in Danger." 2010.

[39] *Mayan languages*. (2014, October 31). Sam Noble Museum - The Sam Noble Museum at The University of Oklahoma Inspires Minds to Understand the World through Collection-Based Research, Interpretation, and Education; Sam Noble Museum. https://samnoblemuseum.ou.edu/collections-and-research/ethnology/mayan-textiles/mayan-textiles-background/mayan-languages/

1,200 different indigenous languages organized into 180 linguistic families spoken in the Americas before European arrival.[40] California had 86 native languages. Currently, the U.S. claims that around 167 indigenous languages are spoken.[41] Mexico currently has a larger group with 282 living indigenous languages.[42] Mexico has been credited with having locations where certain areas, such as north of the Isthmus of Tehuantepec, containing so much linguistic diversity would be "hard to match on [the] entire continent of the Old [European] World."[43] Guatemala has 24 indigenous languages, 22 of which are Mayan languages, and the remaining two are Garifuna and Xinca.[44] About one-third of Mesoamerica speaks Mayan languages, and two of the thirty Mayan languages have died.[45] Although we will zone in on the Mayan Mam language within this complex world of indigenous languages, it is critical to note the cultural importance that each one holds.

Evolving from Proto-Mayan and Mamean languages thousands of years before Spanish colonialism, where it became altered and suppressed with Spanish colonial policies, and then subject to a recent civil war ending in 1996, the Mam community has been in resistance and migration. This migratory diaspora of Mam speakers includes many students living and learning in Californian, and Oakland-based classrooms. With the growing student body of Mayan-Mam-speaking students in the Oakland schools, there is a lack of academic historical text on the history of Mam as a language. Mam Grammar text and Guatemalan histories exist, but what is missing is a *history of Mam as a language*. Borrowing from linguistic

---

[40] Charles G. Mann, "1491: *New Revelations of the Americas before Columbus.* 186.

[41] T. Andrews, (2020, February 25). A brief history of Native American languages in the US. *Interpreters and Translators, Inc.* https://ititranslates.com/blog/a-brief-history-of-native-american-languages-in-the-us/

[42] Clifton Pye, "Documenting the acquisition of indigenous languages." 456.

[43] Ibid.

[44] *Language data for Guatemala.* (2020, February 10). Translators without Borders. https://translatorswithoutborders.org/language-data-for-guatemala

[45] Terrence Kaufman, Terrance. "Aspects of The Lexicon of Proto-Mayan and It's Earliest Descendants." Chapter 4 in Aissen, Judith, et al., editors. *The Mayan Languages,* 63.

studies, anthropology, and history, utilizing leading academic linguistic text,[46] grassroots local media articles, and several one-on-one interviews with native Mam speakers. This book is a humble attempt to start the process of writing such a history from the perspective of those linked to or living it.

With many Mayan linguistic academics to mention, some key authors stand out for their research: Lyle Cambell's historical notes on the Mayan languages, Terrance Kaufman's on mapping early Proto-Mayan languages, Nora England's writings on the grammar of the Mam language and Wesley M. Collins on the centeredness of Mam from a linguistic-cultural perspective.[47] The study of history, referred to as historiography, has many developed histories in European languages. Mayan languages up to date, including Mam, have yet to have a history written on them, a looming yet profoundly important task for historians.[48] This work is an Oakland-centered viewpoint documenting *The history of Mam as a language*, helping both the Mam speaker and non-Mam speaker better understand the complex and powerful history Mam embodies as a language.

---

[46] Terrence Kaufman, Clifton Pye, Lyle Cambell, Barbara Pfeiler, Pedro Lateo Pedro, Nora C. England, Judith Aiseen, Roberto Zavala Maldonado are key linguistic academic authors on the Mayan language.

[47] Lyle Cambell, "Mayan History and Comparison." Chapter 3. Kaufman, Terrance. "Aspects of The Lexicon of Proto-Mayan and It's Earliest Descendants." Chapter 4 England, Nora "Mam" Chapter 19 in Aissen, Judith, et al., editors. *The Mayan Languages*.

[48] For example, see Tore Janson et al. *A Natural History of Latin Tore Janson;* Translated and Adapted into English by Merethe Damsgård Sørensen and Nigel Vincent. (Oxford University Press, 2004).

Miguel states, "I know people here in Oakland and Guatemala that speak other Mayan languages. I speak Mam, but I know others who speak K'iche', and the languages aren't so different. It only gets complicated because some words from Mam can have a completely different meaning when used in K'iche'."

BUBBLE THOUGHT 1 Miguel reflects on the different Mayan languages.

QUESTIONS FROM CHAPTER I:

"SORRY, I NO SPEAK ENGLISH."

1) How have historical US policies influenced the prevalence of English over a multi-linguistic environment?

2) How does the age of Proto-Mayan compare to that of Latin?

3) What is the relationship between Mam and Proto-Mayan in terms of linguistic evolution?

4) What distinguishes the development of European language histories from that of Native languages like Mam?

5) Why are the histories of Native languages, such as Mam, often described as undeveloped?

6) What is the purpose of the book mentioned in relation to the history of Mam as a language?

ANCIENT HISTORY OF MAYAN LANGUAGE

FIGURE 4 Mayan Temple 1, Tikal Guatemala

---

[49] M. Cartwright, (2015). Maya architecture. *World History Encyclopedia*. https://www.world-history.org/Maya_Architecture/

FIGURE 5 Mayan glyphs in the Palenque site museum, Palenque, Chiapas, Mexico.

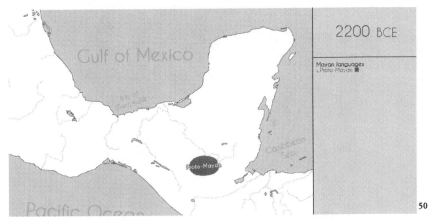

FIGURE 6 Linguistic Map showing Proto-Mayan in 2,200 BCE.

---

[50] YouTube, The History of the Mayan Languages, available at https://www.youtube.com/watch?v=mBxEMGR2jNY

To appreciate the origin of the Mam language, it is imperative to consider the grassroots of the Mayan language before its division. The Mayan languages we interact with today has been revealed to have been a derivative of the Proto-Mayan language dating back no less than five thousand years ago.[51] Linguists have theorized that the Proto-Mayan language was spoken in the Cuchumatanes Mountains of Guatemala around 2,200 to 2,400 BCE. Reconstructed vocabulary of Proto-Mayan speakers has been highly successful agriculturalists.[52] Corn, or Maize, was central to their agricultural practices. Proto-Mayan language included words for material culture, commerce, spirituality and religion, and social organization.[53] The writing aspect of the Mayan language is historically impressive. Anthropologist Dennis Tedlock frames the historical land-scape, "if we apply a narrow definition of writing, demanding that it record the sequence of sounds in a spoken language, we cannot get around the fact that writing existed in the Americas long before Europeans brought the roman alphabet here. Mayans started writing when English (even Old English) had yet to be born."[54] The Mayan languages date back thousands of years, encapsulating social and cultural history long before European arrival. Understanding languages historically should be part of how we learn the ways in which human knowledge was obtained and used in the past, including the language used for math, astronomy, economics, and engineering. Mayan society had developed these disciplines well before Spanish colonialism.

---

[51] Lyle Cambell, "Mayan History and Comparison." Chapter 3. in Aissen, Judith, et al., editors. *The Mayan Languages*, 44.

[52] Ibid,, 54.

[53] Ibid,, 54.

[54] Dennis Tedlock, *2000 Years of Mayan Literature*, 1.

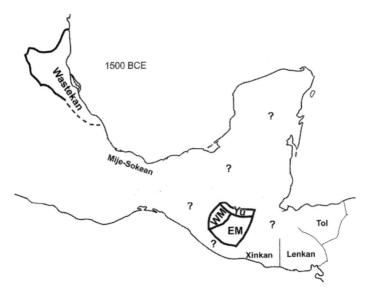

FIGURE 7 Map of Mayan Languages 1,500 BCE.

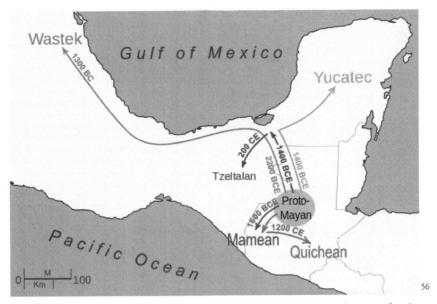

FIGURE 8 Approximate migration routes and dates for various Mayan language families.

---

[55] Terrance Kaufman, "Aspects of The Lexicon of Proto-Mayan and It's Earliest Descendants." Chapter 4 in Aissen, Judith, et al., editors. *The Mayan Languages*, 70.

[56] Terrance Kaufman, "Archaeological and Linguistic Correlations in Mayaland and Associated Areas of Meso-America." *World Archaeology*, vol. 8, no. 1, 1976, 101–18.

Proto-Mayan diversified around 4,200 years ago, with the Huastecan language leaving its mother family first, going down to the Usimacinta River, and developing its own language.[57] Yucatecan Mayan migrated around 3900 BCE, then moved to the lowlands around 3,500 BCE. Eastern Mayan branched off 3,600 BCE. This group would later form the two languages, Greater K'ichean and Mamean, around 3,400 BCE. For the next thousand years, these two languages would continue to diversify.[58] Huastecan shares several sound changes with Ch'olan-Tseltalan and Yucatecan, with many linguists putting them into the same subgroup.[59] However, the Huastecan grammar and lexicon, the vocabulary of a person, language, or branch of knowledge, is so different that it probably broke free from Proto-Mayan for a long time.

The grand scope of the influence and connections Proto-Maya produced over 30 languages and potentially influenced other native nations is immense and not something that should be disregarded. The degree of such influence is still discussed amongst scholars and researchers, with many theories being forwarded of a larger, vast native network throughout Mesoamerica and beyond, to which the Mayans were linked.[60]

---

[57] Lyle Cambell, "Mayan History and Comparison." Chapter 3. in Aissen, Judith, et al., editors. *The Mayan Languages,* 54.

[58] Ibid.

[59] Ibid, 45.

[60] Ibid,, 54.

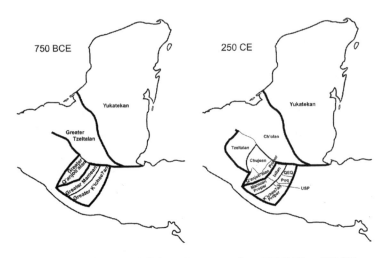

FIGURE 9 Map of Mayan Languages from 750 BCE to 250 CE.

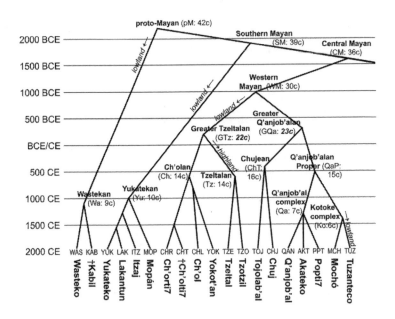

FIGURE 10 Diversification of Western Mayan Languages

---

[61] Terrance Kaufman. "Aspects of The Lexicon of Proto-Mayan and It's Earliest Descendants."
Chapter 4 in Aissen, Judith, et al., editors. *The Mayan Languages,* 71.
[62] Ibid, 66.

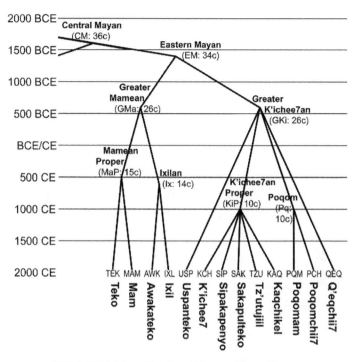

FIGURE 11 Diversification of Eastern Mayan Languages.

For a quick comparison regarding how old the languages are, Latin, the ancestral language of Spanish, created 47 languages. Mayan created 32. Latin is 2,700 years old, while Mam is 2,600 years old, and Proto-Mayan is about 5,000 years old. Mam evolved from Mamean, becoming one of Guatemala's two most spoken indigenous languages, currently surpassed only by the Quiché/K'iche language. The Mam language was closely bonded to the K'ichean from the onset until one thousand six hundred years of the Mayan language's existence, after which it broke off to stand on its own. The most common Mayan language is Quiché/K'iche, which has a rich literary legacy. The book *Popul Vuh* was written in Quiché/K'iche, and Nobel Prize recipient Rigoberta Menchú also speaks Quiché/K'iche.[64] Miguel writes, "I heard that Quiché was one of the main Mayan languages, a relative in

---

[63] Ibid, 67.

[64] Clifton Pye and Barbara Pfeiler, "The Acquisition of Directionals in Two Mayan Languages", 1.

Guatemala told me." Its speakers are Mayan indigenous and located in the southwestern regions of Guatemala. It evolved from the Quichéan lingo well over three thousand years ago, forming their own divisions and further dialects beneath each divide. The distinctions are notable in simple idiolects, speech habits, and accents, identifying each speaking group uniquely.

With over thirty distinct yet related languages forming the Mayan family, the Mamean speakers fell under the Eastern branch. The K'ichean and Mamean languages were closely related and evolved apart over time. Mamean proceeded to generate Mam, along with three closely linked tongues, namely Teko, Awakatek, and Ixil.[65] It is widely understood that the origin of all distinctive languages spoken by the Mayans date back to four thousand years ago when the point of dispersion was most relevant in a region which was only slightly north of the present-day Mam territory.[66] Huastec and Ch'ol have a language system where children attain more verbs, describing actions, whereas children learning Q'anjob'al, Mam, and K'iche produce more noun words, like a person, place, or thing.[67]

[68]

FIGURE 12 Six pages of the Dresden Codex
Pages (55–59, 74) on eclipses (left), multiplication tables, and a flood (far right)

---

[65] Lyle Cambell, "Mayan History and Comparison." Chapter 3. in Aissen, Judith, et al., editors. *The Mayan Languages,* 44.

[66] Mam Maya (no date) *eHRAF World Cultures.* Available at: https://ehrafworldcultures.yale.edu/cultures/nw08/summary

[67] Clifton Pye, "Mayan language acquisition." Chapter 2. in Aissen, Judith, et al., editors. *The Mayan Languages,* 22

[68] Dresden Codex dates back to The *Dresden Codex* is a Maya book, which was believed to be the oldest surviving book written in the Americas, dating to the 11th or 12th century.

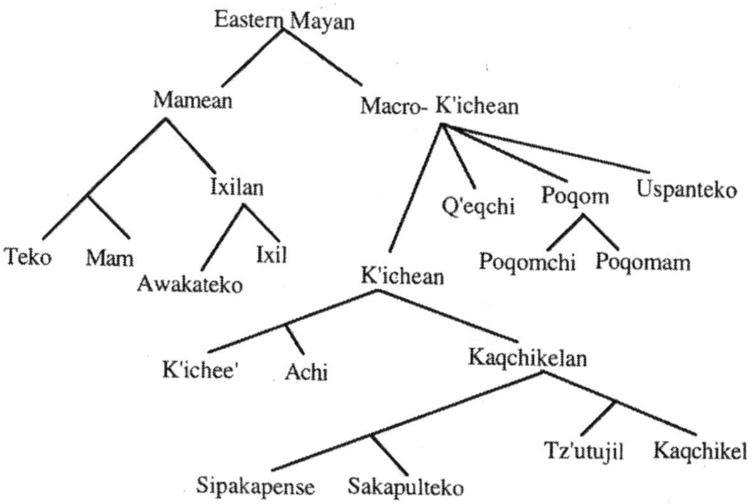

FIGURE 13 Map of Eastern Mayan Languages.

The Mayan writing was sophisticated, used on stone etched Stelae, surrounded by a community that was multi-linguistic. Linguists Karen Dakin and Sergio F. Romero suggested colonial Maya elites in highland Guatemala preserved an archaic form of Nahuatl that was learned before the Aztec state from early connections and trade.[70] Writing helped preserve linguistic knowledge. The entire Mayan writing system was characterized by inscriptions, particularly for official documentation such as contracts and identification certificates. The rulers of Palenque, a major Mayan region of the classic times, left records depicting this unique style dating across nearly half a millennium. Their inscriptions were most active between the years 400 - 800 CE.

---

[69] Rusty Barrett. "The Effects of K'ichean/Mamean Contact in Sipakapense." 25.

[70] Laura Matthew and Sergio F. Romero. "Nahuatl and Pipil in Colonial Guatemala: A Central American Counterpoint." *Ethnohistory* 59 (2012), 765-783.

71

FIGURE 14 Stone Stela, the Mayan writing system,
was formed between 600 and 800 CE.

The monument above is a stela. One of the monuments was carved and erected, made of limestone, in the Mayan region, Belize, most often between 600 and 800 CE.[72] The one pictured was conducted on one side

---

[71] *Stela*. (n.d.). The British Museum. Retrieved December 29, 2023, from https://www.britishmuseum.org/collection/object/E_Am1928-Q-79

[72] Parsons, Lee Allen. "The Origins Of Maya Art: Monumental Stone Sculpture Of Kaminaljuyu, Guatemala and the Southern Pacific Coast." *Studies in Pre-Columbian Art and Archaeology*, no. 28, 1986,. i–216. http://www.jstor.org/stable/41263466. Accessed 18 Feb. 2024.

of the monument to depict the ruler as elegant and royal, while the other side bore hieroglyphs read in a bi-column format downwards from the top left.[73] It contains approximately 112 glyph blocks. The entire Mayan region is filled with such stelae. Pusilha in Belize alone is home to forty of them, each telling its own story. Often, the hieroglyphs spoke about warfare that occasionally raged among the communities in the Mayan region. They would communicate such text as *"k'ik'iy"* which translates to "blood was shed." It is clear that society has been a strong pillar for the Mam and the Mayan people in general for a long time.[74] Some researchers have found advanced mathematics inscribed in the Stelaes, including clear applications of the number zero.[75]

Mayan mathematics was based on a 20-count system that was integrated into their three interlacing and astronomically advanced calendars. It is not clear how the different Mayan languages changed when it came to applying Mayan mathematics, astronomy, hydrology, and botany. Mayan had a syllabic writing system that paired with their physical environment. The symbols representing consonant-vowel pairs or vowels were arranged in glyph blocks to sound out each word. In each glyph block, the symbols were read from top to bottom and from left to right.

[76]

FIGURE 15 Glyph blocks used for Mayan writing.

[73] Aissen, Judith, et al., editors. *The Mayan Languages.*

[74] Ibid., 45.

[75] Anna Blume, "Maya Concepts of Zero." 52.

[76] "Maya Glyphs." *Jaguarstones.com*, https://www.jaguarstones.com/maya/glyphs.html. Accessed 19 Feb. 2024.

Reading Mayan differed from our current Western approach of reading of right-to-left where movements of words composed of sentences and paragraphs. In short inscriptions, the glyph blocks were arranged horizontally or vertically in single-line sentences. Glyph blocks were often placed into a grid with the glyph blocks read from top to bottom and left to right in paired columns.

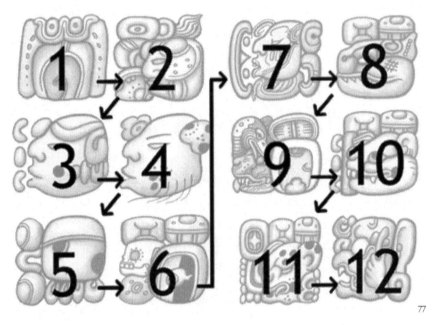

FIGURE 16 Grid-like layout of glyphs that represent numbers.

Mayan mathematics was developed using a zero-to-19-counting 20 based counting system. The Western decimal count system is based on a ten-count system. The Mayan system is based on a 20-count, which is called a vigesimal system. The word vigesimal is rooted in Latin. Twenty in Latin is *viginti,* and in Spanish, *veinte.* The Maya system differs as it starts with 0 and ends with 19. Below are the numbers 0 to 19, utilizing only three symbols: a unique symbol for 0, a dot for one, and a line for five. Our western mathematical system is based on 10, called a decimal system. But things get confusing when you look at inches to a foot, minutes to an hour, hour to a day, we can see many systems are not operating on a decimal system. The Mayan mathematical system was consistently based on a 20 count system, with 400 and 8,000 being important numbers being built off 20. The Mayan calendars utilized 260 and 360 days as key cycles of time, both being divisible by 20.

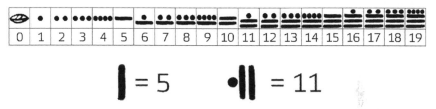

FIGURE 17 The Mayan numeral system is up from 0 to 19.

FIGURE 18 Chichén Itzá
(often spelled *Chichen Itza* in English and traditional Yucatec Maya) was a large city built by the Maya people of the Terminal Classic period. The site is located in Tinúm Municipality, Yucatán State, Mexico.

---

[78] Photo of Chichén Itzá at night, a key location for Mayan Astronomical knowledge.

Chichén Itzá is a key location for astronomical and scientific knowledge grounded in Mayan culture. Gerardo Aldana's *Calculating Brilliance: An Intellectual History of Mayan Astronomy at Chich'en Itza* weaves archeology, mathematics, and astronomy into a cohesive history.[79] "Ancient Mayan civilization was 'obsessed with time'" explains Aldana, "priests controlled ceremonial centers, and all citizens were humble farmers, coming together at temples to participate in astronomically and calendrically determined rituals"[80] Aldana pushes history forward "expanding the scope of the community of discussion around indigenous science." Aldana hopes to "provide new spaces for our ability to represent ancient Mayan scribes, their communities, and their collective endeavors."[81] This history of Mayan astronomy gives a framework for an intellectual environment for the Mayans.

Aldana makes intellectual breakthroughs in explaining the Venus Table and astronomical explanations of Venus within an astronomically focused part of the "Dresden Codex." The Dresden Codex is one of the remaining Mayan books in a German library in the city of Dresden. Aldana looks at the history of scientific writings in the Dresden Codex and offers a new perspective combining a cultural understanding of the Mayan societal practices, generating a closer cultural and linguistic understanding. This also allowed him to have a sharper scientific analysis of what was articulated and accomplished in recorded Mayan astronomy.

[79] Gerardo Aldana y Villalobos, *Calculating Brilliance : An Intellectual History of Mayan Astronomy at Chich'en Itza / Gerardo Aldana y Villalobos.* (The University of Arizona Press, 2021).
[80] Gerardo Aldana y Villalobos, *Calculating Brilliance : An Intellectual History of Mayan Astronomy at Chich'en Itza / Gerardo Aldana y Villalobos.* 23
[81] Gerardo Aldana y Villalobos, *Calculating Brilliance : An Intellectual History of Mayan Astronomy at Chich'en Itza / Gerardo Aldana y Villalobos.* 23

FIGURE 19 Tzolkin Mayan Calendar 260 day cycle

Mayan anthropologist Dennis Tedlock states, "The known history of the Mesoamerican divinatory calendar began around 700-500 BCE when it first appeared at a Zapotec site in the Mexican state of Oaxaca."[83] There are three interlacing Mayan calendars: The *Haab*, the *Tzolkin*, and the *Long Count*, all used together to calculate the days and count the time in the Mayan Calendar. They each have different characteristics and are used for separate purposes.

---

[82] Miguel writes, "I have one of these at home."
[83] Dennis Tedlock, *2000 Years of Mayan Literature*, 13

FIGURE 20 Chichén Itzá during the day and up close.

Western Guatemala has been the home of Mam speakers for around two thousand six hundred years since the point of their emergence as distinct speakers from the K'iche. Like all other civilizations, the Mayan Mam developed a social, political, cultural, and economic structure of their own. There were heads for each town, courts for the settlement of disputes, and social constructs such as marriage and war. The cities boasted the finest architectural designs, and it was no wonder that the rulers felt the urge to erect monuments or stelae to mark their presence and preserve the political history of the Mam.

Lorena interviewed family friend Rudy, a 30-year-old native Mam speaker from Guatemala who resides in Oakland, CA, United States. Reflecting on his knowledge of Mam, Rudy stated, "I was told that the language had its origin in the Cuchumatan Mountains archaeological site for more than 2,000 years."[84] Rudy's findings potentially correlate with Kaufman's Mayan linguistic history research.[85]

---

[84] Lorena interviewed Rudy on 26 November 2023.

[85] Terrence Kaufman, "Archaeological and Linguistic Correlations in Mayaland and Associated Areas of Meso-America." *World Archaeology*, vol. 8, no. 1, 1976, 101–18,.

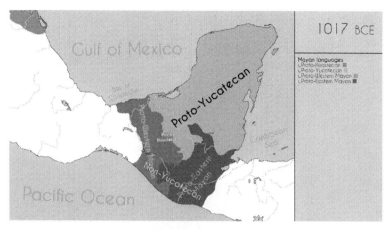

FIGURE 21 Linguistic map of Mayan languages 1017 BCE

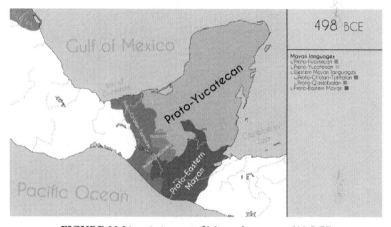

FIGURE 22 Linguistic map of Mayan languages 498 BCE

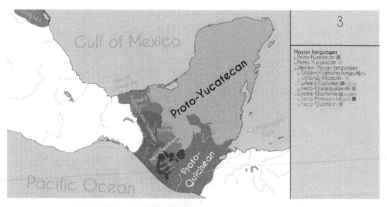

FIGURE 23 Linguistic map of Mayan languages 3 AC

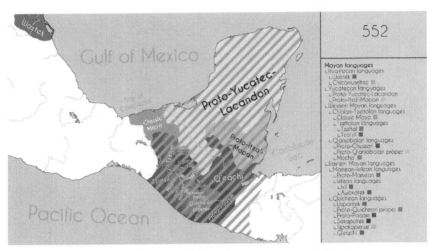

FIGURE 24 Linguistic map of Mayan languages 552 AC

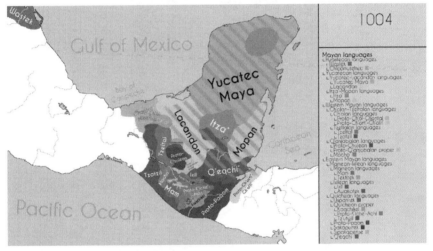

FIGURE 25 Linguistic map of Mayan languages 1004 AC

QUESTIONS FROM CHAPTER 2:

ANCIENT HISTORY OF MAYAN LANGUAGE.

1) How does the way the Proto-Mayan language changed over time help us understand what life was like for ancient Mayans, including how they farmed and what they believed in?

2) How did Proto-Mayan spreading out and evolving affect other ancient societies in Central America, and what can it tell us about how connected those societies were?

3) How does the age of the Mam language compare to other languages like Latin?

4) What are stelaes and what role do they play in the Mayan language?

5) How is Mayan mathematics different from western math?

3

SPANISH COLONIALISM

FIGURE 26 Montezuma meets Cortés in 1519, Unknown artist.

C hristopher Colombus meeting the Taino indigenous in 1492 was a wa-
tershed moment in human history. Historians refer to the exchanges
between the Indigenous, European and African as the Columbian ex-
change. A widespread transfer of plants, animals, precious metals, culture

---

[86] Unknown Artist, (2016, July 2). *Montezuma meets Cortés*. World History Encyclopedia.
https://www.worldhistory.org/image/5277/montezuma-meets-cortes/

and knowledge, was exchanged all throughout the 15th and 16th centuries. The 16th century was the point in time when the Spaniards were spreading their colonial policies across the Americas. Their motivation was to spread Christianity and amass wealth, both of which would accord them effective control in the areas they subdued. The colonial aspirations for wealth, precious metals, and land drove a process of dispossession toward indigenous societies which included Mayans.

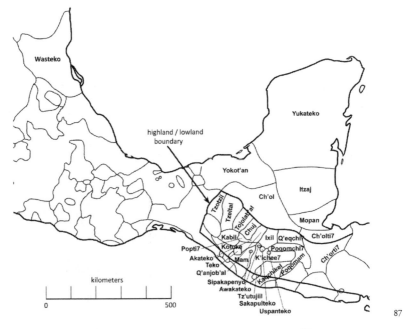

FIGURE 27 Map of Mayan Languages in 1500 CE

Howard Zinn's first chapter in his book *A People's History of the United States* explores this early period of colonial conquest. "In Peru, that other Spanish conquistador Pizarro," Zinn explains, "used the same tactics, and for the same reasons—the frenzy in the early capitalist states of Europe for gold, for slaves, for products of the soil, to pay the bondholders and

---

[87] Kaufman, "Aspects of The Lexicon of Proto-Mayan and It's Earliest Descendants." Chapter 4 in Aissen, Judith, et al., editors. *The Mayan Languages*, 64.

stockholders of the expeditions, to finance the monarchical bureaucracies rising in Western Europe, to spur the growth of the new money economy rising out of feudalism." Howard Zinn goes on to explain that "Karl Marx would later call this process "the primitive accumulation of capital."[88] In his book *Rural Guatemala, 1760-1940,* historian David McCreery continues to analyze Guatemala from the view of this process, "[the] intent here is to examine the history of the process of primitive accumulation in rural Guatemala." Starting in the 1700s and continuing into the 1940s, this primitive accumulation process was in operation, separating Mayans from their land. According to McCrery, from the 1500s to the 1700s, the Spanish state utilized taxes and tributaries to extract wealth from the Mayans.[89] Separating Mayans from the land became a central aspect in forming the necessary conditions for a profitable agribusiness in this earlier time period. One of the driving factors of change in this time period were the Pandemics.

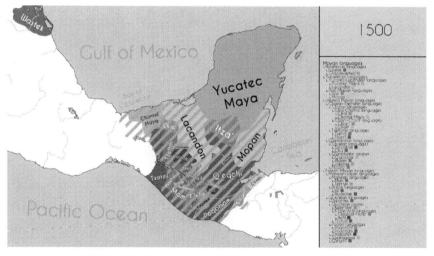

FIGURE 28 Linguistic map of Mayan languages 1500 AC

---

[88] Zinn, *A People's History of the United States,* 12.
[89] McCreery. *Rural Guatemala,* 1760-1940, 3.

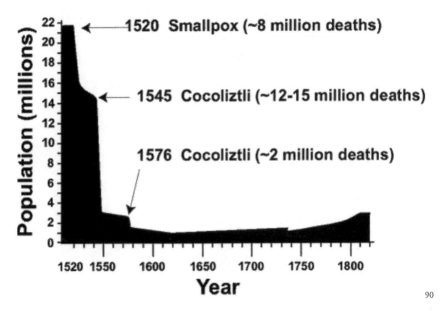

FIGURE 29 Epidemic Map of Early Colonial Mexico, New Spain.

The introduction of foreign bred Pandemics killed millions of indigenous in the 1500s, reshaping the Americas. This destroyed many indigenous civilizations in large waves. Smallpox was devastating to all of the Mesoamerican indigenous nations, killing millions. Historians point out that the epidemic of cocoliztli from 1545 to 1548 "killed an estimated 5 million to 15 million people, or up to 80% of the native population of Mexico."[91] Beyond the pandemics, the Mam community was exposed to forced labor and unfavorable economic conditions under the oppressive 'encomienda system.' This system facilitated the objectification of the Mam, depriving them of their dignity and many other human rights, such as proper working conditions, healthcare, and freedom.[92] Reflectively, his-

[90] Rodolfo Acuna-Soto et al. "Megadrought and megadeath in 16th century Mexico."

[91] Ibid.

[92] Lorena writes, "I heard from a family member that the encomienda system, granted by Spanish colonists to Native American leaders, was abused, leading to the Laws of Burgos which is a law that people can't call indigenous people by names in a racist way and they were aimed at reforming the system. Also, Spanish overlords disproportionately targeted women and children for abuse."

torian of Science David S. Jones comments, "Euroamericans are the benefi-ciaries of the deaths of tens of millions of American Indians; Africans were enslaved and brought to the Americas to provide labor as Indians died."[93]

The Mayan-Mam at the time were in the Western parts of Guatemala and Southern Mexico, and both areas would be in the line of the Spanish colonial advances. Spanish Conquistador Hernán Cortés, who led the Spanish conquest of New Spain, granted a permit to Captains Gonzalo de Alvarado and his brother, Pedro de Alvarado, to conquer current-day Guatemala and El Salvador. Alvarado at first allied himself with the Kaqchikel nation to fight against their traditional rivals, the K'iche (Quiché) nation. Alvarado attacked the K'iche (Quiché), described as "the most powerful and cultured," and violent battles ensued.[94] Alvarado wrote to Hernán Cortés, "And as I knew then to have such a bad will towards service to His majesty, and for the good and peace of this land, I burned them and ordered the city burned and leveled to the ground because it so dangerous and so strong that it seems more like a house of thieves than [the abode] of people."[95]

Alvarado later turned against the Kaqchikel and eventually brought the entire region under Spanish domination.[96] By this stroke, the doors were flung open for a flood of Spanish forces to subdue the surrounding regions, including that of the Mam speaking people. Bernal Diaz reported, "There were burned all the royal archives; all the chronicles of their ancient things; and also the other things which were like literature or stories were destroyed."[97] The Mayans had huge libraries of books as well as hiero-glyphic writings, which were destroyed in mass. The region was also potent

[93] David S. Jones, "Virgin Soils Revisited," *The William and Mary Quarterly*, Oct. 2003, 715.
[94] Delia Goetz, *Popol Vuh. English*. 3.
[95] Ibid, 4.
[96] "Lienzo de Quauhquechollan Exhibition." *Utmesoamerica.org*, The Mesoamerica of the University of Texas. https://utmesoamerica.org/lienzo-de-quauhquechollan-exhibition. Accessed 18 Feb. 2024.
[97] Frank Waters, Frank. *Mexico Mystique The Coming Sixth World of Consciousness*. The Swallow Press Incorporated. 1975, 23.

for its resources, while the colonial settlers sought gold and other precious metals. The Spanish began to establish their systems and slowly expand their influence, with a determined focus to squeeze out the indigenous culture that was predominant before their arrival, thus taking more control.

Spanish Fray Alonso Ponce's expedition led him to the Maya of the Yucatán in 1586 in an event which was described in Mayan history books, written ceremonies, and calendars written in bark, and "only the priest of the idols understood these letters and characters."[98] Bishop of Chiapas, Bartolomé de las Casas, also described Mayan historians that covered religion, founding villages and cities, how kings and lords carried out their deeds, how they elected governors, the history of past leaders, wars, and ancient customs. "[These] chroniclers kept account of the days, months, and years," writes de las Casas, "although they did not have writing such as ours, they had, nevertheless, their figures and characters."[99]

The Spaniards made active strides in assimilating the natives into the Spanish colonial systems, significantly affecting their way of life. Their imposition of Christianity meant that the local religious and cultural practices were frowned upon and even prohibited, to certain extreme extents, with harsh consequences in the event of their continued propagation and practice. Taking away their culture and religion and exposing them to foreign diseases was a move that heavily exploited the Mam, and their numbers began to dwindle. Anthropologist William F. Hanks pointed out an important policy, under-recognized by historians, called *lengua reducida,* which translates into the "reduced tongue." Hanks' article "Birth of a Language: The Formation and Spread of Colonial Yucatec May" points to historians lacking recognition of how the Spanish colonial project *reducción* was in stopping native language usage. As Hanks explains, the Spanish attempted to achieve their conquest through what the Spanish "called *reducción,* from *reducir,* meaning to convince, to reorganize, or to

---

[98] Goetz, Delia, *Popol Vuh. English.* 7.
[99] Ibid.

subjugate."[100] *Reducción* engaged in evangelizing the Maya people, changing the language to Spanish. Hanks explains that the *reducción* had specific linguistic goals: to "eradicate Maya ritual speech and destroy the written text that seemed to record it."[101] A Christian police and inquisition courts existed to enforce such policies.

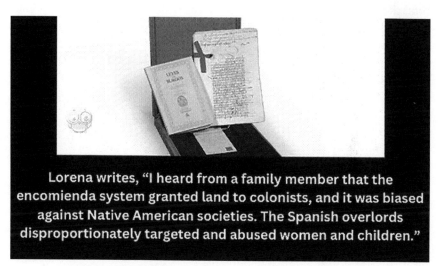

Lorena writes, "I heard from a family member that the encomienda system granted land to colonists, and it was biased against Native American societies. The Spanish overlords disproportionately targeted and abused women and children."

BUBBLE THOUGHT 2 Lorena reflects on Spanish colonialism.

Mayan writing was effectively under attack, and Mam linguistic specialist Nora England asserts, "Mayan writing was effectively abolished by the Spaniards in their campaigns for religious conversion and the elimination of what they deemed to be pagan."[102] Miguel wrote "basically, Spaniards believed that any other religion or culture other than theirs is not a real thing and that's why they believed in converting others into their beliefs." Pagans were understood as a religious, spiritual way of life before Christianity, although this is not the current definition. The most ambitious work by the Spanish Catholics was known as the *Florentine*

---

[100] F. William Hank, "Birth of Language: The Formation and Sprtead of Colonial Yucatec Maya" 450.

[101] Ibid.

[102] Nora England, To Tell a Tale: The Structure of Narrated Stories in Mam, A Mayan Language." 207.

Codex, originally titled *The Universal History of the Things of New Spain*, completed in 1569 by Spanish Franciscan friar Bernardino de Sahagún.[103] This important text covers Aztec, Mayan, and Indigenous culture, economics, natural history, ecology, agriculture, and plant-based knowledge. Notably, historian Eloise Quiñones Keber remarked, "one of the most remarkable accounts of a non-Western culture ever composed."[104] Once this mega-historical work was complete, in 1575, The Spanish Council of the Indies banned all scriptures in the Indigenous languages and usage of medicines, advancing colonial control.[105]

Several Mayan languages have written responses to the earliest Spanish contact. Such contact altered the Mayan languages in many ways, with a merging process where Spanish and Mayan languages mixed.[106] The elimination of Mayan writings increased the role of its oral history. "Mayan languages," explains Linguist Nora England, "have instead had a robust tradition of oral narratives that are learned, practiced, and handed down generation to generation."[107] The fires had a devastating impact on these sacred libraries that covered history, astronomy, science, medicine, math, and mythology.

Anthropologist Rosalva Aída Hernández Castillo reports that the Mam community did not inhabit the *Pueblos de Indios*, an established town recognized by the Spanish crown. As a result, the Mam community, under colonialism, was "diasporic and diffuse." As early as 1526, many Mames were working in the Spanish colonial Cocoa plantations,

---

[103] Jeanette Favrot Peterson and Kevin Terraciano (eds.). *The Florentine Codex : An Encyclopedia of the Nahua World in Sixteenth-Century Mexico / Edited by Jeanette Favrot Peterson and Kevin Terraciano.* First edition. University of Texas Press, 2019)

[104] H. B. Nicholson, "Fray Bernardino De Sahagún: A Spanish Missionary in New Spain, 1529-1590," in *Representing Aztec Ritual: Performance, Text, and Image in the Work of Sahagún*, ed. Eloise Quiñones Keber (Boulder: University of Colorado Press, 2002).

[105] The *Florentine Codex* is now held in the Laurentian Library of Florence, Italy, only accessible in pieces for researchers.

[106] Lyle Cambel, "Mayan History and Comparison," Chapter 3 in Mayan Languages, 52.

[107] Nora England, "To Tell a Tale: The Structure of Narrated Stories in Mam, A Mayan Language." 207.

extracting cocoa beans to Europe. Castillo states the pandemics and exploitative labor systems "killed almost all indigenous Mam populations."[108] Some surviving Mames fled to the Sierra Madre mountain range. This range runs from Chiapas, Mexico, through Guatemala, El Salvador, and Honduras. It also houses many volcanoes.

Shortly after, in the 1700s, the "humanitarian side" of Spanish colonialism in Guatemala was represented by Father Ximénez, an accomplished linguist. He studied the Mayan languages and worked hard to convert the indigenous to Christianity.[109] Ximénez helped the generation of Mayan stories, which, with such interactions, attained the Mayan book *Popol Vuh,* which means Book of the Community, in his parish, which was written in Quiché Mayan. Ximénez translated it into Spanish under the title *Historias del Origen de Los Indios de Esta provincia de Guatemala.*[110] The original book in Quiché has unknown whereabouts. Ximénez describes how Mayans had written books of their own histories, hidden from Spanish authorities. Ximénez was determined to transcribe these different Mayan nations' mythology, tales, and histories. Many Mayans learned to write in Spanish but kept their historical writings secret from Spanish authorities. Ximénez describes a doctrine in the Popol Vuh that seemed to run deep, "first imbibed with their mother's milk, and all of them knew it almost by heart."[111] Ximénez has a comments on the issues of Mayan history and its works, "because I have seen many historians who write about these peoples and their beliefs, say and touch upon some things contained in their histories which were only scattered fragments since the historians had been seen the actual histories themselves, as they were written." Ximénez continues "I decided to put here and transcribe all of their histories, according

---

[108] Rosalva Aída Hernández Castillo, "Cross-Border Mobility and Transnational Identities," 69.

[109] Goetz, Delia, *Popol Vuh. English,* 4-5.

[110] Delia Goetz, *Popol Vuh. English.* 5.

[111] Ibid, 6.

to the way they had written them."[112] The religious, political agenda of Ximénez admits, "this work of mine attempts to give information on the errors, which they had in their paganism and which they still adhere to among themselves."[113] Such work both preserves and destroys the life of the language.

Wesley Collins, a linguistic anthropologist, explains how *Popul Vuh* represents a "perfect balance and order," which is becoming an unreachable but driving goal in our living world. This sophisticated literature stands shoulder to shoulder with other Western canonical texts. The *Popol Vuh* reports four attempts to make humankind, the last being successful, with corn being the basis of life. Prophetically, *Popol Vuh* even states, "Learn to protect yourselves by keeping our secret."[114]

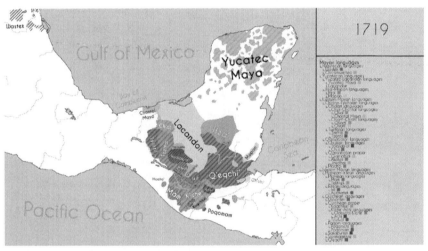

FIGURE 30 Linguistic map of Mayan languages in 1719 AC

All the Mayan books were burned except for four: the religious *Popul Vu* and three astronomical knowledge-centered books with references to even older Mayan books. These were the "Dresden" Codex,

---

[112] Ibid.

[113] Ibid..

[114] Rigoberta Menchú, *I, Rigoberta Menchú : An Indian Woman in Guatemala*, 1

held in Germany. The "Madrid" Codex was held in Spain, and the "Grolier" Codex was held in Mexico. The Dresden Codex received its name from Johann Christian Götze (1692–1749), German theologian and director of the Royal Library at Dresden, who purchased the Mayan Codex in 1739 while traveling to Italy.[115] The "Madrid" Codex was linked to the Extremadura province of Spain, where Hernan Cortez and many *conquistadores* are from. The *Museo Arqueológico Nacional* acquired the Mayan Codex from book collector José Ignacio Miró in 1872. Miró claimed to have purchased the Mayan Codex in Extremadura, Spain, with the theory that one of the conquistadors brought it back.[116]

The Grolier Codex is also called the Maya Codex of Mexico. In 1965, Mexican collector Dr. Josué Sáenz went to the Sierra Madre near Tortuguero in Tabasco State, where he was shown the Codex. He purchased the Codex and let Mayan scholar Michael Coe display the Codex at the Grolier Club in New York in 1971. Yale published an article referring to the Codex as "the oldest known book in the Americas."[117] In 1976, the US-Mexico Artifacts Treaty was applied to return the Codex to Mexico.[118]

---

[115] Robert J. Traxler and P. Loa, *The Ancient Maya*, 127.

[116] Xavier Noguez, Manuel Hermann Lejarazu, Merideth Paxton;, and Henrique Vela (August 2009). "Códices Mayas" 20-21.

[117] *Authenticating the oldest book in the Americas.* (2017, January 18). YaleNews. https://news.yale.edu/2017/01/18/authenticating-oldest-book-americas

[118] Baltazar Brito Guadarama (2018). "El Códice Maya de México. Códice Grolier". *El Códice Maya de México.* Ciudad de México: Instituto Nacional de Antropología e Historia, 1–14.

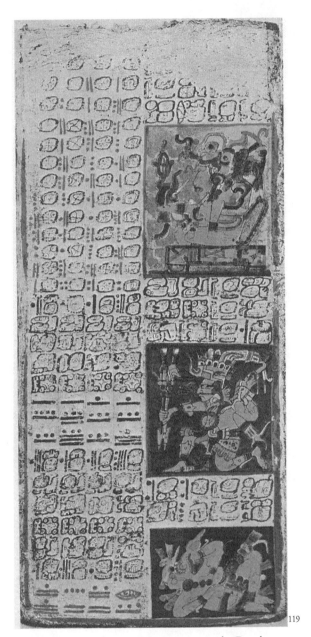

FIGURE 31 Yucatec Maya writing in the Dresden
Codex, ca. 11–12th century, Chichen Itza

[119] The Dresden Codex. [Place of Publication Not Identified: Publisher Not Identified, to 1250, 1200] PDF. Retrieved from the Library of Congress, <www.loc.gov/item/2021667917/>.

The missionary activities targeted the culture of the indigenous people, with missionaries looking to "civilize" the population by converting
the locals into Christians. Instead of maintaining traditional practices,
the indigenous people were introduced to Spanish culture that clashed
with their own norms, and forced to follow them. From a big picture
perspective, Adam Smith remarks on the Americas' colonization in his
Wealth of Nations. "The Commodities of Europe were almost all new to
America," Smith states, "and many of those America were new to Europe.
A new set of exchanges, therefore, began to take place...The savage in-
justice of the Europeans rendered an event, which ought to have been
beneficial to all, [but] *ruinous and destructive to several of those unfortu-
nate countries.*"[120] Those countries today are known as Latin America,
with incredible amounts of gold and silver that had been extracted by
Spain in the 16th and 17th centuries. On another point regarding Adam
Smith, historian Sergia Coffey suggests that Native American cultures
influenced Adam Smith. Coffey points to Adam Smith's favorable view
of labor: "Labor....is the only universal, as well as the only accurate
measure of value" was influenced from "indigenous American economies labor was the most valued factors of production."[121] Reflecting on
indigenous concepts of labor that influenced Adam Smith's *Wealth of
Nations,* reshifts how we understand American economies. Similarly, it
is known that Benjamin Franklin was the most influential Founding
Father, and had close relations with the Iroquois native societies. Many
point to how the Iroquois constitution was one of many key influences
on the US Constitution.[122]

---

[120] Adam Smith, *Wealth of Nations,* 348, emphasis added.
[121] Sergia Coffey "The Influence of the Culture and Ideas of the Iroquois Confederacy on
European Economic Thought" Abstract. 9. (Adam Smith quote, *Wealth of Nations,* 41)
[122] See Johansen, Bruce E.. *Forgotten Founders : Benjamin Franklin, the Iroquois, and the
Rationale for the American Revolution* 1982.

QUESTIONS FROM CHAPTER 3:

SPANISH COLONIALISM

1. How did the colonial policies of the Spaniards in the 16th century impact indigenous societies, particularly the Mayans?

2. What were the primary motivations behind the Spanish colonial conquests in the Americas?

3. Describe the impact of pandemics and forced labor on the Mam community under Spanish colonial rule, and how did these factors contribute to the decline of indigenous populations?

4. Discuss the efforts of Spanish missionaries, such as Father Ximénez, to convert indigenous peoples to Christianity?

5. Explain the significance of the *Popol Vuh* in preserving Mayan cultural heritage despite colonial suppression?

INDEPENDENT
CENTRAL AMERICA

FIGURE 32 Central America's symbol was placed on the flag in 1821
The slogan reads, "United Provinces of Central America."

After breaking from Spain, The Provincial Council of the Province of Guatemala proclaimed the independence of Central America on September 15, 1821. Mexico obtained its independence from Spain that year as well. The next year, some of the countries were annexed into Mexico, only to form (once again) the independence of Central America in 1823. Influenced by the U.S. Declaration of Independence, Mariano de Aycinena y Piñol drafted the Act of Independence of Central America (Spanish: *Acta de Independencia Centroamerica*).[123]

In 1826, the President of the Central American Federation, Manuel José de Arce y Fagoaga, shifted to a conservative party that Mariano de Aycinena y Piñol led. Other key Central American leaders opposed this, leaning towards liberal policies, forming a short civil war from 1826 to 1829. Aycinena led a dictatorship, censored the press, and had a retroactive death penalty. This clashed with José Francisco Morazán Quesada, a liberal Central American politician. Morazán was a general who served as president of the Federal Republic of Central America from 1830 to 1839 and president of Honduras.[124] Morazán was a visionary liberal who made laws for the freedom of the press and freedom of religion, and he actively took power away from the church. The Federal Republic of Central America existed from 1823 to 1841. Political fighting from conservatives, liberals, and separatists lead to Central America's break up. Rafael Carrera, a *cuadillo* conservative Guatemalan politician, was backed by Belgium in 1840 and elected Guatemalan Governor in 1844.

FIGURE 33 Flag of Guatemala (1838-1843)

---

[123] "Documentos de la Union Centroamericana" (PDF). *Organization of American States – Foreign Trade Information System* (in Spanish). Retrieved 12 October 2014.

[124] Christopher Minster, "Francisco Morazan: the Simon Bolivar of Central America" Thoughthco.com. Retrieved 30 August 30 2018 https://www.thoughtco.com/biography-of-francisco-morazan-2136346.

On March 21, 1847, Guatemala declared itself an independent republic, and Carrera became its first president. Historians have differing positions on whether he was a soft ally to the Mayans or not, but he was definitely close to the Catholic church. As one historian states, the "church created a religious justification for the Carrera regime."[125] While Carrera expanded state institutions and developed the young economy, he "facilitated indigenous wage labor."[126] Historian Greg Grandin states, "throughout his long tenure, Carrera would skillfully take advantage of his repute as a defender of indigenous interests to consolidate his power."[127]

Indigenous and Mayan communities had a wave of rebellions across over thirty villages in 1837. Local political autonomy was being abolished by eliminating certain indigenous legal rights. The tense situation, once again, had European influences, with historians pointing to "Liberal reformers discouraged various outward manifestations of Mayan culture."[128] The government adopted Livingston Codes that were meant to abolish special privileges. Borrowing from the 1824 Constitution, they sought to institute equality "without distinction or race." With this in mind, liberal politicians also passed Spanish as the official language with a goal to "extinguish aboriginal tongues," which was nothing short of an attack on the language and culture of the Mayans in Guatemala.[129] There

[125] Reviewed Work(s): Piety, Power, and Politics: Religion and Nation-Formation in Guatemala, 1821-1871 by Douglass Sullivan-Gonzalez Review by: Robert M. Carmack Source: The Annals of the American Academy of Political and Social Science, Nov., 1999, Vol. 566, The Social Diffusion of Ideas and Things (Nov., 1999), 169-171

[126] Reviewed Work(s): Piety, Power, and Politics: Religion and Nation-Formation in Guatemala, 1821-1871 by Douglass Sullivan-Gonzalez Review by: Robert M. Carmack Source: The Annals of the American Academy of Political and Social Science, Nov. 1999, Vol. 566, The Social Diffusion of Ideas and Things (Nov. 1999), 169-171

[127] Greg Grandin, *The Blood of Guatemala*, 103.

[128] Reeves. *Ladinos with Ladinos, Indians with Indians*, 2

[129] Greg Grandin. *The Bloodshed of Guatemala*, 101

existed a leftover influence of Spanish elitism which was mixed with the modern liberal arrogance of the politicians who led the independence process. Rigoberta Menchu reflects on this period, explaining how on "October 13, 1876, President Rufino Barrios signed Decree No. 165, a law that took away the legal identity of the indigenous people there and turned them into *ladinos.*"[130] Barrios expropriated communal indigenous lands, which fostered a new Mam community in Chiapas, Mexico.[131] On December 15, 1883, the government of General Porfirio Diaz instituted the Colonization law, helping establish indigenous-based settlements, including in Chiapas, where a Mam community lived, leading to Mexican citizenship.[132]

Miguel writes, "Newer generations of Mayan youth are slowly forgetting the Mayan-Mam way of living, that includes forgetting the traditions and customs of the past. For example, teens are now using modern day clothes, instead of traditional clothing their parents and grandparents used to wear."

BUBBLE THOUGHT 3 Miguel reflects on the changing cultural customs moving away from their Mayan origin.

[130] Menchu Rigborta Menchu, *Crossing Borders*, 17

[131] Hernández Castillo, Rosalva Aída. "Cross-Border Mobility and Transnational Identities," 69.

[132] Ibid, 71.

FIGURE 34 Map of Guatemala in 1829.
Note that borders with Mexico, Yucatán, and Chiapas are not defined.[133]

---

[133] John Lloyd Stephens; Catherwood, Frederick. *Incidents of travel in Central America, Chiapas, and Yucatán.* (London, England: Arthur Hall, Virtue and Co., 1854)

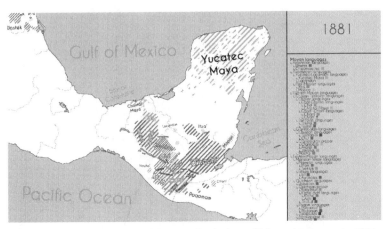

FIGURE 35 Map with stripes showing the decline of Mayan languages in 1881.

Different Christian denominations sought translations of the bible. Anthropologists have looked at how the "Bible use among Mam evangelicals who belong specifically to the Presbyterian denomination."[134] The first evangelical denomination to gain official governmental permission to work in Guatemala was in 1882. Among Presbyterians, a translation of the Gospel of John was completed in the K'iche language in 1923. The entire New Testament, as translated by Dora Burgess and Patricio Xec, was completed in 1947. Among the Mam, a hymnal song of praise appeared in 1927, and the New Testament of the Bible was done in 1939.[135]

FIGURE 36 Flag of Guatemala in 1924.

---

[134] Mathews C. Samson. *"The Word of God and 'Our Words:' The Bible and Translation in a Mam Maya Context."* Chapter 4. 66.

[135] Ibid, 68.

Economic activities would also seem to favor the assimilated Mam, which pushed many people away from the indigenous culture, often inadvertently. It became more and more difficult to get people interested in matters of culture as it seemed to be a dead-end for those looking to pursue a livelihood. The younger generation was, therefore, increasingly pursuing the Spanish systems, which ultimately affected lifestyle, cultural orientation, and social interaction.

Guatemala generated 50 ruling families that dominated the private sector in the 1920s, economically based on agricultural exports and ruled by military force.[136] At this time, 400 German business owners owned half of the coffee exports, while about 1,000 elite Guatemalans owned the rest of the Coffee farms. This is rooted in earlier developments the country faced. David McCreery's article Debt Servitude in Rural Guatemala 1876-1936 explains, "Debt peonage flourished in late nineteenth- and early twentieth-century Chiapas, Yucatan, and Guatemala, a consequence of rapidly expanding demand for raw materials in the industrial North Atlantic states."[137] McCreery continues to explain that the state worked with landlords in a debt servitude situation, where farm workers owed money to the landlord and were paid very little in return, while exports would be shipped to the United States.

The 1930s was a difficult period for indigenous communities in the area. In El Salvador in 1932, the Nahua indigenous communities had a revolt against the government that was violently crushed, called the *Matanza,* the massacre in Spanish. Thousands of Nahua died, targeted by the government. Such government-targeted practices pressured the Nahua community to stop using the Nawat language in public spaces, and they stopped exhibiting their traditional clothing.

Chiapas, Mexico, also suppressed indigenous cultures. The Governor of Chiapas (1932-36), Victoriano Grajales, prohibited Mames from wearing traditional clothing or speaking Mam. This prohibition included schools. One

---

[136] Tom Barry, *Roots of Rebellion Land & Hunger in Central America.* p. 54.

[137] David McCreery, "Debt Servitude in Rural Guatemala, 1876-1936." *The Hispanic American Historical Review*, vol. 63, no. 4, 1983, pp. 735-, https://doi.org/10.2307/2514903.

Mam student reported, "It was then when the teachers came to the schools that our language was prohibited: if you spoke the Tokiol (Mam language), the teacher would punish you. This is why we lost the Mam [language]."[138]

The movement towards independence was incomplete for the indigenous communities. Even though the power of Spanish colonialism would disappear its policies would continue through many of the states and governments of Central America. Even up until the recent period, the Guatemalan state has historically continued policies that are disadvantageous, hostile, and oppressive to indigenous communities with the civil war ending all the way up to December 1996.

QUESTIONS FROM CHAPTER 4:
INDEPENDENT CENTRAL AMERICA

1   Discuss the political conflicts between conservative and liberal factions in Central America during the 1820s and 1830s, focusing on the roles of Mariano de Aycinena y Piñol and José Francisco Morazán Quesada.

2.   Analyze the impact of Rafael Carrera's presidency on Guatemala, particularly in relation to indigenous communities and the Catholic Church.

3.   How did liberal reforms in Guatemala during the 19th century, such as the adoption of Spanish as the official language and the implementation of Livingston Codes, affect indigenous populations and their cultural practices?

4.   Explore the role of religion, particularly evangelical Christianity, in influencing indigenous cultures and languages in Guatemala, considering factors such as Bible translations and economic activities.

---

[138] Rosalva Aida Hernández Castillo, "Cross-Border Mobility and Transnational Identities." p. 72.

5

20TH CENTURY GUATEMALA

FIGURE 37 This painting by Diego Rivera, "Gloriosa Victoria," tells the story of the 1954 overthrow of the democratically-elected Jacobo Arbenz government. Coup Colonel Carlos Castillo Armas greets Secretary of State John Foster Dulles, who holds a bomb with the face of Eisenhower, surrounded by people who were murdered in the coup. U.S. ambassador John Peurifoy is to his left, with military officers and CIA director Allen W. Dulles whispering in his brother's ear. On the right, the archbishop of Guatemala, Mariano Rossell Arellano, blesses the act while Guatemalans protest.

Guatemalan history is deeply intertwined with the United States, especially looking at what happened in 1954. Juan González, author of *Harvest of Empire: A History of Latinos in America,* explains, "A garrison state for more than forty years, Guatemala was home to the longest

---

[139] "June 27, 1954: Elected Guatemalan Leader Overthrown in CIA-Backed Coup." *Zinn Education Project.* González, Juan. Harvest of Empire, 135-137.

and bloodiest civil war in Central American history. The roots of that war go back to an almost-forgotten CIA-sponsored coup in 1954, which overthrew a democratically elected president."[140] Guatemalan presidents worked for landlords' interests as well as the American-owned United Fruit Company. This was the case for President Jorge Ubico, who ruled from 1931-1944. Ubico convinced many Mayan communities to work on government projects in place of paying taxes. "He made all Indians carry passbooks and used vagrancy laws to compel them to work for the big landowners."[141] United Fruit Company investments made incredible profits from the arrangement.

In 1944, a coalition of professionals, teachers, and officers, many inspired by Franklin D. Roosevelt's social democratic policies, launched a movement to change Guatemala. Once the unions backed up this coalition, Ubico was forced to resign. This opened up what historian Juan González calls Guatemala's "first democratic election."[142] Juan José Arévalo, a university philosophy professor, author, and majestic speaker, was elected. Arévalo was succeeded by Jacobo Arbenz Guzmán, a military officer and disciple of Arévalo's leadership who was elected in 1951. Arbenz redistributed unused lands to many campesinos, benefiting many members of the Mayan community with his land reforms. Guatemala at that time had a seventy (70) percent illiteracy rate and eighty (80) percent of the countryside had challenging conditions, making the question of land in Guatemala a central issue. Two (2) percent of the landholders owned seventy-two (72) percent of the arable land.[143] When Arbenz passed Decree 900, a new law which ordered the expropriation of all unused property that was larger than six hundred acres. This land was distributed to peasant farm worker families. Historian Greg Grandin contextualizes why this is so significant, "[not] only did the agrarian reform present a direct threat

---

[140] Juan González, *Harvest of Empire*, 135.

[141] Ibid.

[142] Ibid., 136.

[143] Ibid.

to the near absolute power wielded by the agro-bourgeoisie since 1871, but for the first time in Guatemalan history a significant amount of state authority was used to promote the interests of the nation's disenfranchised masses."[144] The response to Decree 900 is so immense it will forever change Guatemala's politics and the Mayan indigenous's living conditions.

In 1954, out of 341,000 landowners, only 1,700 were affected by Decree 900, but this included the United Fruit Company, owning 600,000 (mostly unused) acres.[145] Arbenz offered The United Fruit Company officials $1.2 million as compensation, which was rejected, and The United Fruit Company officials wanted $16 million for their land. When the Guatemalan president and the United Fruit Company officials could not agree, the Secretary of State John Foster Dulles and the CIA Director Allen Dulles convinced President Eisenhower, in the words of Historian González, "that Arbenz had to go."[146] "Operation Success" was launched with authorization from American President Eisenhower and the mechanics were organized by the CIA.

Guatemala colonel Carlos Castillo Armas was the one who led the coup which was financed and trained in Nicaragua. The U.S. quickly recognized the new regime, and Castillo repaid his sponsors. Castillo outlawed five hundred trade unions and returned more than 1.5 million acres to United Fruit Company and other big landlords. Historian Greg Grandin exerts a bold position regarding this incident, "There is a general consensus today among academics and Guatemalan intellectuals that 1954 signaled the beginning of what would become the most repressive state in the hemisphere." Many scholars point to the Guatemalan state being "responsible," as Grandin comments, "for the torture and murder of two hundred thousand of its citizens" in this period.[147]

Castillo's government shifted economics and exports which led to

---

[144] Grandin, *The Blood of Guatemala*, 200.
[145] González, Juan. *Harvest of Empire*, 137.
[146] Ibid.
[147] Grandin, *The Blood of Guatemala*, 198.

a positive change in finances. Between 1960 and 1974, exports grew on a tremendous scale. $75 million worth of goods were exported in 1960, increasing to $173 million in 1974. Cotton trade figures jumped from $6 million to $71 million in the same time frame. Sugar sales went from $0.1 million to $50 million in export, and meat from 0.2 million to $22 million. The top five majorly exported crops grew from $105 million in exports to $368 million in exports, one of the highest in Latin America.[148]

In 1970, the International Labor Office reported on Guatemalan agricultural work conditions. It found working conditions to be subhuman, and the working and lodging conditions totally unacceptable with widespread contagious diseases. In 1973, The National Teachers Union launched a strike to challenge some of the conditions of impoverishment. The strike spread throughout the country.

QUESTIONS FROM CHAPTER 5:

20TH CENTURY GUATEMALA

1. How did the 1954 coup in Guatemala impact the country's political landscape and social fabric, particularly in relation to land reform and the indigenous Mayan community?

---

[148] Carmack, *Harvest of Violence*, 14.

THE GUATEMALAN
CIVIL WAR

Lorena writes, "From what I heard, the reason the Guatemalan guerrillas had a war with the Guatemalan government was because they were against the rich people taking from the poor. This took place in Ixca, Quiche and Huehuetanango. It started with ten people, including leaders from Todos Santos Cuchumatán where my family is from."

BUBBLE THOUGHT 4 Lorena reflects on the origins of the Guatemalan civil war.

The impacts of the 1954 coup shaped the future of the country. The Guatemalan Civil War was considered to start in 1960, only six years after the coup. It ended in 1996, lasting longer than their Nicaragua and El Salvadoran counterparts. Nicaragua had a revolution in 1979 overthrowing the long US backed dictatorship ruled by the Somoza family going back to 1936. Lead by the Sandinistas National Liberation Front (Spanish: *Frente Sandinista de Liberación Nacional* "FSLN," and

El Salvador had a twelve year communist lead guerrilla war led by the Farabundo Martí National Liberation Front (Frente Farabundo Martí para la Liberación Nacional) "FMLN." The Salvadoran peace accords were in 1992 ending the civil war, bringing the FMLN and the Government into agreements that led to a shift into the electoral arena. Nicargua had a proxy war with the Sandinistas in state power against the *Contras*, a counter-revolutionary army backed by the recently overthrown Somoza family and US forces. *Contras* engaged in counter-insurgent practices to destabilize the Nicaraguan Sandinista regime. The civil war and political fighting within El Salvador and Nicaragua slowed down and for the most part ended in the early nineties. While Guatemala's civil war continued until 1996, lasting a bit longer. The war largely between peasant and farmworker-based organizations, many of them Mayans, on the one side, and the Guatemalan government and its military, who still served the interest of the wealthy landlords and American corporations, on the other.

FIGURE 38 Pictured: Antonia Choc with her grandson

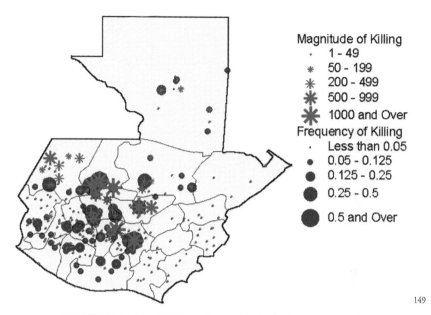

FIGURE 39 Map of Killings during the Civil War in Guatemala.

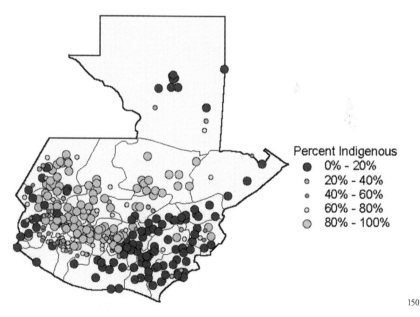

FIGURE 39 Map of Indigenous Populations in Guatemala.

---

[149] Timothy R. Gulden. "Spatial and Temporal Patterns in Civil Violence: Guatemala, 1977–1986." *Politics and the life sciences* 21, no. 1 (2002): 26–36.
[150] Ibid..

During the height of the civil war in 1984, there was a conference of Guatemalan hosted by Bishops. It was titled *To Build a Peace*, in which a collective letter was written stating, "[one] of the greatest richness of Guatemala and one which giver her a special face in the concert of nations is the plurality of indigenous cultures evident in the different ethnic groups which populate Guatemala."[151] The indigenous were under political attack, suspected of being part of a revolutionary organization by military personnel. In the 1980s, you could feel the political - military tension. The fight was between the government and military of Guatemala, backed by the U.S., against rebel guerrilla fighters and organizations, many being indigenous. The war involved heavy brutality, human rights abuses, and horrible massacres, as well as resistance.[152] Scholar Timothy R Gulden analyzed spatial patterns of violence in Guatemala from 1977 to 1986, shaping the civil war. Gulden states, "state carried out most of the killing during the conflict in an ongoing campaign of repressive terror involving the military, the police," notably referencing "semi-autonomous 'death squads' and state-organized civilian 'civil patrols.'"[153]

Most people worked hard during the civil war, as work conditions were tough. But there were always signs of resistance. In February 1980, 70,000 cane cutters, 4,000 cotton pickers and coffee pickers went on strike demanding living wages. The government raised the minimum wage from $1.12 to $3.20 a day, responding to the pressures of such a strike.[154] Mam were part of these strikes, they would look for work in the cities, with language being the central barrier. But during the civil

---

[151] Carmack, *Harvest of Violence*, 3.

[152] *Guatemala - countries - office of the historian*. (n.d.). State.gov. Retrieved December 8, 2023, from https://history.state.gov/countries/guatemala.

[153] Timothy R. Gulden. "Spatial and Temporal Patterns in Civil Violence: Guatemala, 1977–1986." *Politics and the Life Sciences*, vol. 21, no. 1, 2002, 26–36, https://doi.org/10.1017/S0730938400005736.

[154] Carmack, *Harvest of Violence*, 20.

war there was an added suspicion that if you are indigenous, you are viewed as supporters of rebel organizations, making them targets of the government attacks.[155]

Political scientists have linked massive killings to the indigenous targets during the Guatemalan civil war, "over half of the killing took place in municipalities in which the Mayans made up between 80 and 90 percent of the population. This is remarkable because such municipalities make up less than 8% of the municipalities in the country and house just over 8% of the total population."[156] The government would often blame state sponsored violence on rebel indigenous organizations. Cutipa-Zorn investigated Guatemalan General Rios, who launched a counterinsurgency operation called "Plan Victoria" that included "Techo, Tortilla y Trabajo" (Housing, Tortilla, and Work). This operation would launch a plan called "Frijoles y Fusiles" (Beans and Bullets), offering beans to highland indigenous Mayans for cooperation or death if they chose not to cooperate.[157] In that vein, Shelton H Davis and Julie Hodson wrote an important book called *Witnesses to Political Violence in Guatemala*, based on the personal testimonies of 115 missionaries and researchers. The authors concluded that "the army killed thousands of innocent people" and "there is no indication that the guerrillas terrorize and massacre the civilian population as is frequently claimed by the Guatemalan government."[158] Scholar Gavriel Cutipa-Zorn writes on the roots of "authoritarian internationalism" in Guatemala. Guatemala's indigenous localized productivity, including farming for their own food, was "aggressively" changed to a "monocultural" productive

---

[155] R. Nolan (n.d.). *Guatemalan Child Refugees, Then and Now (disponible en español)*. NACLA. Retrieved December 31, 2023, from https://nacla.org/news/2021/04/23/guatemalan-child-refugees-then-and-now-disponible-en-espa%C3%B1ol

[156] Timothy R. Gulden. "Spatial and Temporal Patterns in Civil Violence: Guatemala 1977-1986.", 6.

[157] Ibid.

[158] Carmack. *Harvest of Violence*, xi.

system, the commercialized coffee production system.[159] Rigoberta Menchú Peace Prize winner describes coffee work in her famous autobiography, *I, Rigoberta Menchu.*

> I worked from when I was very small, but I didn't earn anything. I was really helping my mother because she always had to carry a baby, my little brother, on her back as she picked coffee. It made me very sad to see my mothers face covered in sweat as she tried to finish her work load, and I wanted to help her. But my work wasn't paid, it just contributed to my mothers work.[160]

Beyond the work conditions were the political conditions, which were just as challenging.

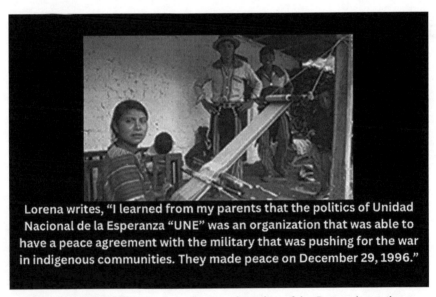

Lorena writes, "I learned from my parents that the politics of Unidad Nacional de la Esperanza "UNE" was an organization that was able to have a peace agreement with the military that was pushing for the war in indigenous communities. They made peace on December 29, 1996."

BUBBLE THOUGHT 5 Lorena reflects on the ending of the Guatemalan civil war.

---

[159] Gavriel Cutipa-Zorn, "Israel, Guatemala, and the Agricultural Roots of an Authoritarian Internationalism." *Cultural Dynamics*, vol. 31, no. 4, 2019, 350–64, https://doi.org/10.1177/0921374019860941.

[160] Rigoberta Menchú,. *I, Rigoberta Menchú : An Indian Woman in Guatemala,* 33.

Rigoberta Menchú, in her autobiography, wrote, "I must say before I start, I never went to school, and so I find speaking Spanish very difficult. I didn't have the chance to move outside my own world and only learned Spanish three years ago."[161] Rigoberta Menchu voiced her experience of massive indigenous massacres in Guatemala. The U.S. was not neutral in this war and actively supported the government and helped train government-linked death squads who were on the frontline of killing suspected rebels in Both Guatemala and El Salvador.[162]

By 1996, when the war in Guatemala was coming to an end, the bloodshed was so extreme that journalists asked the question of whether this should be considered genocide.[163] Martin, a Mam native speaker, moved to Oakland when he was four years old and explained, "[m]any families fled Guatemala in the '80s to Mexico and the States because of the genocide," Martin explained.[164] Historian Greg Grandin concludes in his book *The Blood of Guatemala* with this key fact, "Faced with unprecedented challenge to their authority, the state, the military, and the oligarchy, supported United States, identified Indians as the collective enemy and launched a wave of repression that the United Nations - administered Truth Commission has characterized as genocide."[165] In 2013, United Nations High Commissioner For Human Rights court, has charged Guatemalan "former de facto head of state, José Efraín Ríos Montt, for genocide and crimes against humanity."[166]

---

[161] Ibid.,1.

[162] Greg Grandin.. *The Last Colonial Massacre.* 187-188. and Chomsky, Noam. *Turning the Tide : U.S. Intervention in Central America and the Struggle for Peace.* 1985.

[163] Jo-Marie Burt "From heaven to hell in ten days: the genocide trial in Guatemala." In *Guatemala, the Question of Genocide,* 11-36. Routledge, 2018.

[164] Jose Martinez, CBS News. "Community in Oakland's Fruitvale District works to save ancient Guatemalan language." Sept 27, 2023.

[165] Greg Grandin, *The Blood of Guatemala,* 233.

[166] PRESS RELEASES OFFICE OF THE HIGH COMMISSIONER FOR HUMAN RIGHTS: Pillay welcomes historic genocide judgment in Guatemala, 13 May 2013.

FIGURE 41 A sign in Guatemala that reads Wanted José Efraín Ríos Montt for genocide in the 1980s.

MAYAN LANGUAGE DEVELOPMENTS UNDER CONDITIONS OF WAR

The continuity of Mayan linguistic resilience: What is remarkable historically is how communities continued to make positive linguistic progress amid such challenging conditions, demonstrating incredible resilience. The language Mam would develop in its own unique ways in reflection of the difficult social conditions. These military regimes had deep negative impacts on the Mam community in the 1950s all the way up to the end of the civil war in 1996, but that does not mean there weren't important Mam-related linguistic developments taking place. The 1960s brought a resurgence in Mam and Indigenous studies. In 1969, the Spanish School Proyecto Lingüístico Francisco Marroquín

(PLFM) was formed, which helped train Mayan language development, including preparing dictionaries of many Mayan languages.
This included a Mam dictionary, published in the 1980s,[167] written by
Native Mayan speakers. In 1987, the Academia de Lenguas Mayas de
Guatemala (ALMG) formed a single alphabet for the Mayan languages
of Guatemala.[168] These ALMG alphabets do not fit and connect with
all dialect variations of the Mayan languages. PLFM launched the
OKMA, Oxlajuuj Keej Maya' Ajtz'iib,' a linguistic research group that
"flourished" for nineteen years, creating new Grammar works in Mayan
languages in the 1990s.[169] The adverse cultural situation resulted in the
emergence of local leaders amongst the Mam who worked to preserve
the endangered culture. The initiators of this motion took up the mantle
as educators, advocates, and community-based leaders who rallied the
masses to make strides in protecting and promoting the Mam language
and culture, emphasizing the importance of embracing their origin and
identity.[170] As a result, parallel efforts were made to ensure that, even
as the youth gained knowledge through the Spanish colonial systems,
they would still be able to learn about who they were at their core and
even speak their mother-tongue. To promote this, there have been bilingual education programs, adding that the syllabus is also taught in
Mam. Further, there have been community-based programs that bring
people together on a cultural basis to interact and build meaningful
social bonds.

In 1994, a number of key conclusions were published by the First
Congress of Mayan Education in Guatemala (Spanish: *Primer Congreso
de Educación Maya en Guatemala*). The findings proposed a basic education of the Mayan worldview, including the notion of "fourness."
Fourness engages the completeness of life and the universe, supported

---

[167] Nora England, et al.,. *The Mayan Languages*, 2.
[168] Ibid,. 9.
[169] Ibid, 3.
[170] Ibid.

by four aged *Pawahtuns* (a group of Native Americans), in discussing an old deity who ruled over the days at the end of the year.[171] The theme was unity out of diversity, ideas are not simple, and cooperation, all linked to the notion of "fourness." Collins explains this was driven by the philosophical search for centrality. It was also building an equilibrium between opposing elements within Mayan culture. To conclude, Collins explains, "I believe that all of these notions can be derived from a basic understanding of centeredness."[172] The conference took place two years before the formal ending of the civil war. The civil war ended on December 29th, 1996, after 36 years of fighting when the government signed a peace accord with the Guatemalan National Revolutionary Unity (URNG). A new hope for peace arose from such peace accords. But the difficult economic conditions continued. Immigration from Guatemala to the US did not decrease but increased, and one city in particular became a special new home for many newcomers, Oakland California.

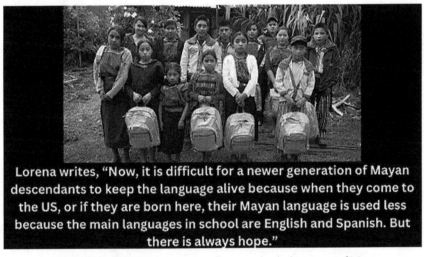

Lorena writes, "Now, it is difficult for a newer generation of Mayan descendants to keep the language alive because when they come to the US, or if they are born here, their Mayan language is used less because the main languages in school are English and Spanish. But there is always hope."

BUBBLE THOUGHT 6 Lorena reflects on the declining use of Mam.

---

[171] Collins, *Maya-Mam*, 90-91

[172] Ibid, 114

QUESTIONS FOR CHAPTER 6:
THE CIVIL WAR

1. In what ways did the exploitation of indigenous labor, such as in the coffee industry, intersect with the broader socio-political dynamics of Guatemala during the civil war era?

2. How did the historical context of the Guatemalan Civil War impact the development and preservation of the Mam language, as evidenced by initiatives such as the formation of linguistic research groups and the publication of dictionaries in the 1980s and 1990s?

3. Discuss the significance of the Academia de Lenguas Mayas de Guatemala (ALMG) in standardizing Mayan language alphabets, and analyze the challenges faced in creating alphabets that accommodate the dialect variations of Mayan languages.

4. How did community-based efforts, such as bilingual education programs and cultural gatherings, contribute to the revitalization and promotion of the Mam language and culture amidst the socio-political turmoil of the Guatemalan Civil War era and its aftermath?

7

OAKLAND

Lorena writes, "Radio B'alam is an organization that has helped the Mayan communities keep in touch with what has been happening around them lately. Besides Radio B'alam, there have been other media support systems who have helped with the Mayan community, some including Paraiso TV, Rigo Mendoza Videos, Raiz Digital Films, Studio Mam Producciones, and many others."

BUBBLE THOUGHT 7 Lorena reflects on Mam media channels in the US

The Los Angeles Times reported, "Oakland is home to one of the largest concentrations of Mam speakers in the nation."[173] Oakland might be the world's epicenter of Mam speakers outside of Guatemala and Chiapas, Mexico. Lorena and Miguel offer insights on why this is the case.

---

[173] Carcamo, Cindy. "Ancient Mayan languages are creating problems for today's immigration courts," Los Angeles Times. AUG. 9, 2016.

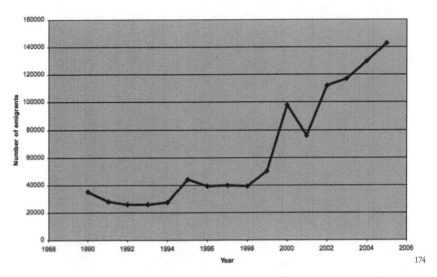

FIGURE 42 Immigration from Guatemala to the U.S. from 1990 to 2005

Lorena writes, "Mayan Guatemalans come to Oakland for a variety of reasons. One of the reasons could be because of their families and how bad the poverty in Guatemala is. The main reason is the possibility of winning papers legally. Many Guatemalan Mayans plan to be able to win their papers and go back to their country and be able to travel back and forth. But unfortunately, it's not easy for every immigrant to win their papers. Some actually get the chance to win their papers easily; it may take them four years or less. But for others it's different, theirs is more years. For example, one of my family members came to Oakland so long ago but never had the chance to get their papers and it's been probably been ten years or more.

Another reason Mayans come to Oakland is because of poverty. Poverty in Guatemala has not gotten any better. Since I went to Guatemala recently, I have had the chance to see the prices in Guatemala. For example, a pair of shoes like sandals is 350 quetzals, which is roughly $45 dollars. But when I went for the first time, a pair of sandals was at least 115 quetzales (the Guatemalan currency, equating to about $10USD) or less. You can

---

[174] Guatemala - Civil War, Human Rights, Refugees. (n.d.). In *Encyclopedia Britannica*.

already see how much the prices have changed, that is why many Mayan people see the possibility of coming to Oakland to earn money and be able to send it to their family over there."

Miguel writes, "Every Year, new Guatemalan residents come to the U.S. I know a handful of them who settle down here in Oakland, CA. But why do they come specifically to Oakland? I asked, and the answers were all different depending on the person. Some said they had family members already settled in Oakland. Others said it was due to the fact Oakland offers a lot of help to those with little to no money, such as food stamps and financial help from the government. Others have said it was because applying for a permanent residency and/or asylum was somewhat of an easy process; the only exception was, in some cases, it took a long time to get them.

Besides these factors, we also need to know why they left Guatemala, and according to the answers I got, most of their motives were due to poverty, which made life over there incredibly difficult. Employment over there is not easy, too, and payment is very low, which is why some Guatemalans decide to move to the U.S. in hopes of a better life. Others have said it was because of life-threatening circumstances; for example, some deny obeying criminals that live near them, so they get threatened and decide to move to the U.S."

The population of Mam speakers in Oakland is reported to be rising continually, currently standing at just short of forty thousand.[175] Many of the people here went in search of asylum due to the atrocities that were propagated against them in their homes. Lorena reflects, "I heard that for some immigrants that come to the U.S. by the hands of immigration, it's easier for them to fight for the asylum/residence, but the ones who don't come by the hands of immigration, it's harder for them to get their papers and have to wait for many years, unlike the ones who come by immigration." As a result a formidable Mam community has grown in Oakland.

---

[175] Jack Spence et al. "Promise and Reality: Implementation of the Guatemalan Peace Accords".

FIGURE 43: Logo for Radio B'ALAM Voces Maya

Radio B'alam has emerged as a critical and important radio station that disperses information in the Mam language. It is based in Fruitvale, Oakland. The program was officially founded on December 11, 2020, and it is the *first* program in the country to broadcast in Mam.[176] The word *b'alam* translates to jaguar and, as Jesus Ayala explains, "is an homage to the Mayan priests who officiated at only the most important ceremonies."[177] Based in Fruitvale, and known for its Chicano movement aura and murals, Ayala comments Fruitvale is "California's second-largest indigenous population, with Latinos and indigenous people comprising nearly 54% of Fruitvale's population."[178] The radio program's founders, Henry Sales and Cresencio Ramirez, are Mam speaking natives from Guatemala and are building a movement to both preserve Mayan languages and to keep indigenous listeners informed. Crecencio Ramirez Pablo, an Oakland-based

---

[176] Jesus Ayala, "Oakland's Mayan Diaspora Overcomes Language Barriers and Finds Refuge in Radio B'alam." 140.

[177] Jesus Ayala, "Oakland's Mayan Diaspora Overcomes Language Barriers and Finds Refuge in Radio B'alam." 140-141.

[178] Ibid.

Mam activist and founder of Radio B'alam stated, "They gravitate to Oakland, he said, because it is a sanctuary city. There are more job opportunities, medical services, and legal resources to apply for asylum."[179]

Mayan immigrants faced much harsher conditions during the Covid lockdown. Showing the importance of Radio B'alam work, one study points to in Alameda county, "Mayan patients had a COVID-19 positivity rate of 72.8% as compared with 27.1% (P < .001) for nonindigenous Latino patients and 8.2% (P < .001) for white patients."[180] Radio B'alam represents an important ethnic media radio, helping the Mam community navigate the difficulties of the U.S. This type of ethnic radio is not new; it is estimated that 60 million people in the U.S. get their news from 3,000 ethnic media organizations in the U.S.

Oakland's Native American Health Center in Fruitvale has a Women, Infant and Children program "PIC," supporting pregnant women and new moms. Ninoska Ayala, WIC program director, estimates that 25% of the program's clients speak Mam. What is difficult is there is very little medical information in Mam.[181] In the past five years, the WIC team has added two Mam speaking health workers to engage the growing number of Mam clients.

Mayan-Mam in Oakland continue to find their home, as their businesses and communities develop in the Fruitvale east Oakland area. Guatemalans are the biggest newcomer student group in the Oakland public schools. It is without a doubt the Mam community and the city of Oakland are developing a tight relationship. Oakland has a long history of embracing those negatively impacted by larger acts of injustices, resulting in conditions for the Mam community to grow.

---

[179] Florence Middleton, "How one health center is serving Oakland's growing Mam community" The Oaklandside, Dec 12th, 2022.

[180] Jesus Ayala, "Oakland's Mayan Diaspora Overcomes Language Barriers and Finds Refuge in Radio B'alam." 143.

[181] Florence Middleton, "How one health center is serving Oakland's growing Mam community" The Oaklandside, Dec 12th, 2022.

QUESTIONS FOR CHAPTER 7:

OAKLAND

1) Why is Oakland a unique city that attracts Maya-Mam migrants?

2) What does Radio B'alam do and why are they important? What are they the first to do?

3) How did COVID affect the Mayan-Mam community more so than other communities?

8

MODERN LINGUISTIC RESEARCH

*"I show that the particular overlap of the cultural
and grammatical theme of centeredness
is specific to Maya-Mam and basic to the Mam conception of the world."*
- Wesley M Collins [182]

Guatemalan Spanish is often referred to as *Castellano* as Miguel mentions. 93% of Guatemalans speak Spanish while it is the native language of only 69% of the population.[183] The brutality of the genocidal civil war tore deep into the fabric of Guatemala. But even in the midst of such horror, important linguistic developments were able to take place. Mam-related linguistic organizations that contributed to Mam's linguistic studies took off. In 2010, Form and Analysis in Mayan Linguistics "FAMLi" emerged, publishing several works on Mayan linguistic systems.[184] In 2000, *Centro de Investigaciones y Estudios Superiores en Antropología Social* "CIESAS" was formed in Mexico. CIESAS produced PhD scholars focused on indigenous languages, including Guatemalan-Mayan-based

---

[182] Wesley M Collins. *The Heart of the Matter: Seeking the Center in Maya-Mam Language and Culture*, 19.

[183] *The World Factbook*, Central Intelligence Agency, 2023-08-29.

[184] England, Nora, Maldonado, Nora Zavala, Aissen, Judith, et al., editors. *The Mayan Languages*, 4.

languages.[185] Even with such developments, schools in Guatemala were Spanish driven.

Spanish was, during this time, the dominant language in Guatemalan schools, and this is still the case in 2024. In 2015, Olimpas Gómez Lopez presented a thesis, "The Maya Mam Language and ethnic identity of the Students" (Spanish: *El Idioma Maya Mam y la Identidad Étnica de los Estudiantes*) to the Department of Education and Licensing of Teachers at the University of San Carlos de Guatemala, the oldest University in Guatemala. The paper argued that the Mam language served as a symbolic force for Mayan culture and Mayan ethnicity, substantially different from other communities. Guatemalan cities employ multiple pressures from schools to workplaces to conform to Spanish as the central language. Parents are no longer involved in teaching the Mayan language to their children for fear that they will be victims of exclusion and discrimination.[186] As a result, in newer generations the Mayan-Mam Language is not used as much, demonstrating a decline in the language.

A small community of linguists and sociologists have specialized in studying Mam in Guatemala, Mexico, and the U.S.. Guatemalan scholar Jose Andrade Gabriel Aguilar wrote his recent thesis on the "Loss of the Mayan-Mam Cultural Identity amongst Students for School Spanish-based Learning." Aguilar comments on how culture and identity are deeply connected, and "culture is a characteristic that defines the identity of a person." Agular explains the "customs and histories that shape a person, their customs and common history. Therefore, it's important to understand that language is inherently an expression of culture and identity." Aguilar points to deeper meanings of language regarding our identity and

---

[185] England, Nora, Maldonado, Nora Zavala, Aissen, Judith, et al., editors. *The Mayan Languages,* 4.

[186] Ely Olimpas Gómez Lopez, *El Idioma Maya Mam y la Identidad Étnica de los estudiantes* Tesis presentada al Consejo Directivo de la Escuela de Formación de Profesores de Enseñanza Media de la Universidad San Carlos de Guatemala. septiembre 2015, 10.

expression, "we are worth transmitting from generation to generation the most intimate part of our being, through language we transmit and express our culture including both the internal and external values and interpretations of our identity."[187] In this case, oral history is used over written history, to pass important information to the new generation.

Guatemalan scholar Ely Olimpas Gómez López wrote his thesis "The Mayan-Mam Language and the Ethnic Identity of the Students," with important recommendations to revive the Mam language. López concludes that teachers "must develop pedagogical activities in the development of classes, using the Mam Language as a basis for reading and writing." Regarding school "educational establishments" López states, "the elements of Mayan Culture in all areas and sub-areas of the curriculum; Give specific talks on the importance of ethnic identity giving the opportunity for Mayan community leaders to share knowledge of the Mayan Cosmovision; and promote socio-cultural activities that include the experience and elements of Mayan culture." López' ambitious goal is "to guarantee the fluent use of the Mayan-Mam Language by young people in diverse environments and situations" while taking into account "the Mayan worldview."[188] As a teacher in Oakland reflecting on López' recommendations, we lack the knowledge and resources, text and tools to be able to offer such education in our classroom. But there can be a shift towards valuing oral history. Both scholars are graduates of the Universidad de San Carlos de Guatemala, the oldest University in Central America, formed in 1676. Universidad de San Carlos de Guatemala has a rich body of linguistic academic work on Mam, that is yet to connect to academic and educational institutions in the US.

---

[187] Jose Andrade Gabriel Aguilar. Pérdida de la identidad cultural maya Mam en los niños por la práctica del idioma castellano en la escuela. Escuela de Formación de Profesores de Enseñanza Media. Universidad de San Carlos de Guatemala. Guatemala, julio de 2016, 26-27.
[188] Ely Olimpas Gómez López "El Idioma Maya Mam y la Identidad Étnica de los estudiantes" Tesis presentada al Consejo Directivo de la Escuela de Formación de Profesores de Enseñanza Media de la Universidad San Carlos de Guatemala. septiembre 2015, 84.

Mam linguistic specialist Nora England explains the importance of an oral tradition, particularly tales, in the Mam language. Tales typically contain five elements: a 'once upon a time' in the introduction, an aspect that marks the stage of an action through its grammar, the mandatory use of quotes, words that carry emotional responses, and invoking traditional knowledge in the conclusion.[189] Together, these form narrative tales central to Mayan-Mam culture and linguistic practices, passing down knowledge and traditions to new generations. This shows how deeply culture is tied to the workings of the Mam language. Nora England is widely cited for mentioning 15 different distinct Mam dialects which are divided into Northern, Southern and Western Mam.[190]

This can get complicated as Mam is not a centralized language containing large internal diversity. Eliseo, a primary school teacher in his early twenties who plays soccer for the Comitancillo selection team, speaks of some of the variations in the Mam language.

> ELISEO: Because in different places there are indigenous people. But their language [he pauses] they pronounce different than the Mam language here. In other words, all the Mam languages are different. They are not all the same.

> JEFF: So the Mam language is different in different places?

> ELISEO: Yes. At the moment of pronouncing the words, the difference is there.

---

[189] Nora England. "To Tell a Tale: The Structure of Narrated Stories in Mam, A Mayan Language." 230.

[190] Simon, Megan, "A Phonetic Distance Approach to Intelligibility between Mam Regional Dialects." 22.

JEFF: For example, the Mam [language] of those in Huehue[tenango] is different?

ELISEO: [M hm] Yes.

JEFF: So then are they the same indigenous pueblo. . .

ELISEO: Yes! [he says emphatically over Jeff's question]

JEFF: . . .Or are they a different indigenous pueblo?

ELISEO: No, it is the same indigenous pueblo.

JEFF: So everyone feels they are the same then, the same Mam Pueblo? ELISEO: M hm [nodding affirmatively].[191]

Miguel and Lorena describe their experiences of meeting native Mam speakers in Oakland and not being able to understand their dialectic. Mam has several dialectics, with several unique particular locally based linguistics adaptations. But there are often keywords that cross over.

Megan Simon's 2019 Master Thesis presented to San Jose State University's Department of Linguistics and Language Development, was titled "A Phonetic Distance Approach to Intelligibility between Mam Regional Dialects." It charts the dialects' degree of difference, looking at what point is there a breakdown in communication. Simon reports on four Mam students in Guatemala, with books written from Huehuetenango or San Marcos when they were first learning to read. "But the books in the schools...are written in another version of Mam, so also you learn the Mam of other regions. Almost all of the books are from other parts, some

---

[191] Jeffrey A. Gardner and Patricia Richards. "The Spatiality of Boundary Work: Political-Administrative Borders and Maya-Mam Collective Identification." *Social Problems (Berkeley, Calif.)*, vol. 64, no. 3, 2017, 439–55

from San Marcos, some from Huehue - it's whoever they contracted to write the book." Another answer stated, "[some books are the dialect from here [San Juan Ostuncalco] There are others that are from Huehue, others from San Marcos." Variation in vocabulary came up as an issue, "[there in Huehue [they say] /wa'/ - it's 'toad'. And here [San Juan Ostuncalco] is /xta'/, so they are different. We had a book that we started to read, and this word came up. 'What is this?' we asked the teacher. Then he told us that it was the same, that they are dialectical differences."[192] Variation is pronounced in the Mam language.

A Mam native and Mam interpreter in California was contracted by the library for translation work. The interpreter commented, "they ask [me] to make flyers in Mam. But it's a little but confuse [sic]. because the people from Todos Santos they can...some of them can read but...if I'm writing something in my Mam, my language, they will not understand. That's the problem."[193] Simon's study outlines the degree of differences, and concludes by stating there are four main dialect groups: Western, Southern, Seleguá, and Todos Santos. Simon offers recommendations of understanding the uniqueness of each dialect.

Nora England states Mam is the most internally diverse of the Mayan languages. With 15 dialects, there are three major groups of the Mam dialects: Northern, Southern and Western. The figure below shows the geography of these three distinct dialects.

---

[192] Simon, Megan, "A Phonetic Distance Approach to Intelligibility between Mam Regional Dialects." 50.

[193] Simon, Megan, "A Phonetic Distance Approach to Intelligibility between Mam Regional Dialects." 50-51.

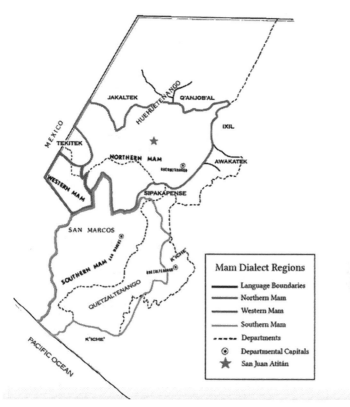

194

FIGURE 44 Differing Mam dialects and their regions in Guatemala

One Guatemalan Mam immigrant farm worker reports a fascinating view of how Mam is practiced in his workplace in Mexico. "At first when they spoke among them in Mam I remained silent; they thought I couldn't understand them," a Mam worker reported. "Truth is, I was ashamed I might not pronounce as well. But gradually I got bolder, and my grandmother's conversations started coming back to me, from when I was a kid and we spoke in tokiol [another name for Mam]...Now we chat and joke with them in *Tokiol, and nobody asks who's from Guatemala or from Mexico; we are the same people,* and we lend each other a hand."[195]

[194] Language revitalization in Oakland: A visual interview with Tessa Scott. (2023, August 21). Social Science Matrix. https://matrix.berkeley.edu/research-article/language-revitalization-in-oakland-a-visual-interview-with-tessa-scott/

[195] Rosalva Aída Hernández Castillo. "Cross-Border Mobility and Transnational Identities.", 77-78.

The joking in a language that transcends borders has a deep meaning of unity and belonging, with memories of the grandmother passing down linguistic gems.

Another Mam immigrant reports their memory of travels. "My grandparents spoke the Mam language, and they come from Guatemala. The origins of all Mam people are in the Tacaná Volcano. Over time, the Mam language stayed in this country [Mexico]; we are all Mam."[196] A community of Mam formed in Chiapas, Mexico, containing important relations with several other indigenous groups and a linkage with their roots in Guatemala.

Linguistics offers us insights into culture. Linguistic anthropologist Wesley M Collins' follows this principle of looking at language to understand culture in the Mam community. In his *The Heart of the Matter: Seeking the Center in Maya-Mam Language and Culture,* Collins' work shows how the Mayan Mam contains a sense of centeredness that shapes cultural and grammatical systems. Reflecting and affirming " this Maya Mam worldview" throughout the structure of the language, which includes its grammar. Collins explains how "[language] and culture comprise a system of life, thought and practice that is worthy of our investment and support."[197] He explains the Mam language has a deep connection to sacred space, forming a center. "Where language and culture come together is in the minds of native speakers," Collins explains, "this emic perspective—local meaning—that I have sought in this study as we have seen how centeredness is realized in cultural and grammatical themes, and conceived of and reflected in talk and life lived out among the Mam themselves."[198] Collins suggests the Mayan-Mam language values centeredness.

Collins builds off of earlier academic work, including Nora England's research on how culture and grammar are tied together. Collins is an

---

[196] Rosalva Aída Hernández Castillo. "Cross-Border Mobility and Transnational Identities.", 4.

[197] Collins, *Maya-Mam.* 39

[198] Wesley M. Collins, Wesley M. "The Center as Cultural and Grammatical Theme in Mam (Maya)." 17–31

ethnographer, someone who is attempting to give the authentic voice of the Mam community, including their actions and ideas. Collins explains, "What I try to do then, as an ethnographer, is attempt to live the life of a Maya-Mam- at least to a limited degree."[199] He consistently explains how grammar and meaning are based on the Mam language. Considering Collins is engaging in ethnography, engaging in in-depth interviews, and valuing the culture as the context for knowledge and linguistics. How does this relate to the history of Mam? Collins explains, "To understand another culture, it isn't enough to simply note their practices...It includes the perspective and practice of history."[200] This includes learning what he calls "cultural knowledge" and, most importantly, understanding "how that knowledge has been appropriately expressed throughout reported history." Finishing his point, Collins states, "Language gives us a powerful tool for understanding and interpreting these norms."[201] Collins concludes that "centeredness is not only a cultural theme, one which continually rises in the thoughts and daily lives of the Mam, it is also an integral part of the language as well."[202]

Collins describes Guatemalan public schools as vehicles to have Spanish absorb Mam. Local public schools are often a twisted type of "bilingual" in Spanish and Mam, using a method called "subtractive bilingualism," where Mam is used "only as a bridge to Spanish, after which the bridge can be burned."[203] Fast forward to modern times, the conditions of the Mam community are still challenging. A press release in 2022 titled, "Mayan-Mam ethnic group, on the verge of disappearing due to lack of government support." The statement said, "The Maya-Mam community of Soconusco has for years been the forgotten and marginalized ethnic group by the authorities of the three levels of government, and despite the

[199] Collins, *Maya-Mam*, 33
[200] Ibid., 19.
[201] Ibid., 19.
[202] Ibid., 152.
[203] Ibid.,.55

efforts of the indigenous people to preserve their culture, customs, and language, they are now in danger of disappearing."[204] Such revitalization efforts should include the global diaspora of Guatemalans, notably the U.S. with Oakland in particular, as important links to the chain.

The Guatemalan big cities, which are cities of commerce, economic institutions, and potential large employers, all operate in Spanish. Mayan immigrant workers are then subject to heavy pressure to adapt to Spanish to gain work and support themselves and their families. Within these conditions, there is also a new wave of professionals who believe that the new generation should learn both Spanish and Mam fluently "without inter-linguistic contamination."[205] This group is leading a revitalization effort, which includes the Maya Language Academy, the Maya Writer's Association, and university and community groups. Building bridges with their Oakland relatives would be an important point of the revitalization efforts, as Mam students in Oakland report "slowly losing" their Mam.

The Maya-Mam perspective is cultural and leads to being a political issue because of oppressive historical conditions. Scholars, Karine Vanthuyne and Marie Christine Dugal, explain in a recent article exploring regenerative Maya-Mam ways of governing, and they found the local Mam political activism was focused on reconstructing *kojb'il* (political-moral community) based on their *conciencia*, or consciousness. This Maya-Mam community challenged corruption within state public funds and demanded a contamination-free environment in relation to mining operations.[206]

There is also a distance between the Mam and hospitals. One study found that there was a lower percentage of deliveries "due to the poor access to formal obstetric health services" and a lack of "trust with communities and

---

[204] Translated by Content Engine LLC. "Maya-Mam Ethnic Group, on the Verge of Disappearing Due to Lack of Government Support." *CE Noticias Financieras*, English ed., ContentEngine LLC, a Florida limited liability company, 2022.

[205] Ibid., 56.

[206] Karine Vanthuyne and Marie Christine Dugal. "Regenerating Maya-Mam Ways of Governing, Indigenous Emancipatory Politics in the Age of the Extractive Imperative." *The Journal of Latin American and Caribbean Anthropology*, vol. 28, no. 3, 2023, 251–60

in local cultural norms and traditional Mam practices."[207] The Mam face challenges that are thoroughly documented within their Guatemalan homeland, causing immigration and forming a large diaspora linked to Oakland.

Guatemala is a difficult environment for language development, as Spanish dominates the workplaces and schools and challenging conditions from the aftermath plague the landscape. Nevertheless, rich linguistic developments have taken place regarding the Mam language. A new generation of Mayan intellectuals, writers, and bilingual leaders are unearthing. The more a new generation learns about their culture, history, language, the more tools they have to reverse engineer the harmful impacts laid out from the past.

---

[207] "Quantitative Methodologies Reveal a Diversity of Nutrition, Infection/Illness, and Psychosocial Stressors During Pregnancy and Lactation in Rural Mam-Mayan Mother–Infant Dyads From the Western Highlands of Guatemala." *Food and Nutrition Bulletin*, 2015, https://doi.org/10.1177/0379572115610944.

GENERAL INTERVIEWS

The following are interviews we did asking Guatemalan native Mam speakers in Oakland what they know about the history of the Mam language. The purpose is to understand how much historical memory there was of the Mam language. The following are interviews which Lorena, Miguel, and Anjelica conducted with Native Mam speakers to learn more about what the community knew about Mam history.

The questions are:

1. How did you learn Mam?

2. Did you learn it as your first language?

3. How much Mam did you use as a little kid, five (5) years old?

4. How much Mam do you use now?

5. What were you told about the history of Mam?

6. Have you heard any stories of the formation of Mam?

7. Are you worried about Mam not surviving as a language?

8. Are there things that you understand in Mam that you cannot articulate in Spanish or English?

9. What made you or your family come to Oakland?

10. Do you still communicate with your family members in Guatemala in Mam?

To assist in painting a picture of the contemporary Mam speakers to-day, interviews were conducted one-on-one, some in Mam and others in Spanish. The results gathered the following information:

1. All of the respondents said that they had learned Mam from their families, with the majority being from parents. One of them said that they picked it up easily because it was the language that those around them spoke.

2. Over 90 percent of respondents listed Mam as their first language. One exception to this said that their first language was Spanish, with Mam following next.

3. Above 80 percent of respondents stated that they used Mam "all the time" as children at the age of five, with one of them saying that they used just 50% of the language by then, while the other 50% was catered for in Spanish.

4. All respondents said that they use Mam all the time these days. One of them gave a caveat by saying that they only use it outside of work since work demands that they employ English more. Many of the interviewees balance Mam in the home and English in society.

5. Two correspondents reported some knowledge about the history of Mam. Rudy stated, " I was told that the language had its origin in the Cuchumatan archaeological for more than 2000 years." He also states, "I didn't hear many stories about the formation; the only fact I know is that it was formed around 4,000 years ago." William responded in Mam that he knew the "basics"..." like I pretty much know some past Mayan leaders for example Tecun Uman, their culture, just the basics." Most correspondents did not report any background knowledge of Mam's history.

6. Less than 10 percent knew something about the formation of Mam, and even then, it was very little. One said that their grandmother told them that the language as spoken today is very different in tone from how it was spoken before. The other said that they knew that it came from ancestors but that this was as far as their information went. Dennis, in Spanish, reported, "Yes, my grandmother told me that the Mam we use now is not the same as the one used years ago. It has changed the way it sounds, and it is spoken. She said that man is a formation of a man that was different, sounded different, and used by our great great great grandparents." This doesn't quite answer the question but represents a historical understanding of the changing language.

7. When asked whether they were worried about the language dying off, over 80 percent responded in the affirmative. The two that responded, on the contrary, argued that there is still a growing desire among people to learn the language, and there are a lot of people already speaking the language at the moment.

8. When asked whether there are things that they understand in Mam but not in either English or Spanish, they all answered in the affirmative. This is really important in thinking about the uniqueness of Mam knowledge that is not translatable.

9. When asked why they moved to Oakland, most of them said that they came to acquire legal status, around twenty percent for asylum, and under 10 percent fleeing poverty conditions in their hometown.

10. When asked whether they still communicate with their families in Guatemala in Mam, they all answered in the affirmative. This demonstrates a live Mam diaspora and network, with communications in Mam as a living operating international language.

The deduction from this survey is that a lot of cultural information is at risk of going extinct despite the fact that the language is still being spoken. The major concern with this is that there will likely come a time when the language may also die as it will not have a solid foundation upon which to stand. The Mam are a beautiful people. Their culture is unique, their language iconic, and their history is ancient. However, it is paramount that the generations to come are exposed to this rich well of knowledge, be they Mam or otherwise. The value that exists in the historical tales of the Mam community holds rich cultural lessons and knowledge that is passed from generation to generation. It carries identity and a sense of belonging. Initiatives such as Radio B'alam in Oakland that look to preserve the language of the Mam are lessons to be borrowed in the practice of its preservation and revitalization.[208] Our interviews show there is very limited historical knowledge of the Mam language, and as some seek to revitalize different aspects of the culture, we can never forget how intricate the history is to the culture. The history of Mam gives us insights into the ancient Mayans, colonialism, modern genocide, immigration, and cultural resilience. This research only scratches the surface and a deeper analysis deserves to be employed.

---

[208] Ayala, Jess. Oakland. n.d. *Mayan Diaspora Overcomes Language Barriers and Finds Refuge in Radio B'alam.*

MIGUEL'S INTERVIEWS

Martiria (Mam)

Since birth, we were taught to speak Mam as our first language. From then on, it was our form of communication between relatives and friends.

Yes, I learned Mam as my first language.

As a little kid, Mam was the only way for us to communicate amongst family members so we used it all the time.

To this day, me and my family still use Mam as our only spoken language at home. We do this so that future generations don't forget about it and keep it alive.

I know for a fact that at some point the language Mam, and the culture around it was at risk of extinction due to colonizers wanting to eliminate it, but other than that I'm not sure.

Not that I am aware of.

I am worried about Mam and the culture not surviving for long because as generations come, they forget to learn it; oftentimes, they even feel ashamed of it, which is one of the reasons it might not survive in the future.

There are some words that we know in Mam that don't really have a specific word in either Spanish or English, but we can also find ways to describe it.

Personally, I came to Oakland because I had friends who settled here.

Yes, I have family back in Guatemala, and yes, I still communicate with them in Mam.

Rosa (Mam)

I learned about Mam through my parents and family members.

Yes, it was my first spoken language.

Used it pretty much a lot.

To this day, I still use Mam a lot.

That there's Guatemalans who can write in Mam, but very few.

Sadly, I haven't heard any stories about the formation of Mam.

I think there's a chance of Mam dying out, but I also believe there's also a chance of it surviving if we keep it alive for the next generation.

Yes.

My sister lived In Oakland when I came, so I decided to stay with her.

Yes, and we always speak Mam.

William (Mam)

I learned it from the family around me.

Yes.

By the time I was five years old, it was pretty much our way of communication.

I use it at home all the time, especially with family.

I only know the basics of it, like I pretty much know some past Mayan leaders, for example, Tecun Uman, their culture, just the basics.

Not that I can remember.

It really depends; I would say it's 50/50 that it will survive and/or die out.

Yes, quite a few.

Family had been here and so we also decided to stay here in Oakland.

Yes, not often, but we communicate still, and yes, it's always in Mam.

Klester (Mam)

I was taught through parents.

Yes, it was the only language spoken.

All the time, no doubt.

I speak Mam often.

Honestly, nothing much. I know some history now that I'm older, but younger, I wasn't taught. much about it.

Not at all.

Yeah, to be honest, my siblings speak English more often at home.

I think so; there are words complicated to translate.

We had friends already here.

Yes, I have family in Guatemala, and we do communicate in Mam.

Josue (Spanish)

I was taught by my parents.

No, it was my second language because I had learned English first.

I would say by the time I was 5, I would use Mam very little. I would mostly understand it just not speak it.

I use a decent amount of Mam. not so often.

Nothing really.

No, I haven't ever.

My guess is maybe, if younger kids aren't taught Mam there's high chances it may not survive, at least not here In the U.S.

A lot, but quite the opposite, there are things in Spanish or English that I do not know how to say in Mam.

My parents just thought Oakland was a good place to live in.

I know my parents communicate with family In Guatemala, mostly in Mam. I don't communicate much because it gets hard to talk with family since Mam isn't my first language.

LORENA'S INTERVIEWS

Lusela (Spanish)

I learned Mam through my parents.

No, I learned it more as my second since Spanish was my first language.

I used a little bit of Mam.

I use the language a lot.

I was told that Mam comes in different versions.

No, I haven't heard any stories.

Yes, because it runs through our family's history.

Yes, there are words that are difficult to articulate in Spanish and English.

My family came to Oakland because of poverty over there in Guatemala.

Yes, I do communicate with them in Mam because they have a better understanding than in Spanish.

Rudy (Spanish)

I learned Mam through my parents since that's the only language they speak fluently besides Spanish.

Yes, I did learn Mam as my first language.

Around five years old, I knew Mam like 50%, I wasn't fluent but was speaking well in where people would understand me.

I use the language all the time since it's my first language.

I was told that the language had its origin in the Cuchumatan archaeology for more than 2000 years.

I didn't hear many stories about the formation. The only fact I know is that it was formed around 4,000 years ago.

No, I am not worried because a lot of people desire to learn this language.

Yes, there are things in Mam that I can't articulate in Spanish or English.

My family and I came to Oakland because in Guatemala, there was a lot of violence, and there was not enough work.Yes, I still communicate with my family in Mam because they don't know a lot of Spanish.

Eliver (Spanish)

I learned Mam from my parents because that's the language they would always communicate with

Yes, I learned it as my first language.

Around five years old, I knew about 50% of Mam.

I use about 80% of Mam because I also speak Spanish for those who don't speak Mam.

I was told that the language Mam is one of the most spoked out of the 23 dialects in Guatemala.

No, I haven't heard any information.

Yes, because the language starts fading away when parents don't speak in their dialect and because there is a mix of Ladinos that start to infer and start speak mainly in Spanish.

Yes, they are words that I can't articulate.

Yes, most of my family members arrived to Oakland because of the poverty in Guatemala.

Yes, I do because they are more fluent in Mam than in Spanish.

Mario (Spanish)

I learned Mam from my parents.

Yes, I learned it as my first language because it was our dialect in Todos Santos.

When I was 5 years old, I knew about 50%.

I use Mam most of the time with all my family, and for those who don't know Mam than, I speak Spanish to them.

I was told that Mam is one of the nine languages that make up the Guatemalan group.

No, I haven't heard about the formation of Mam.

Yes, because most parents who have children born in the U.S. forget to teach them their dialect, and now the kids focus on what is being more spoked which is English and Spanish.

Yes, there are words that can't be articulated in Spanish or English.

Yes, I arrived in Oakland because I heard that there was better financial help for families and since Guatemala was not getting any better.

Yes, I do communicate, Mam, with my family members because it was our only way of communication since we were younger, and that can't be forgotten.

Basilia (Spanish)

I learned Mam from my parents.

Yes, I learned it as my first language because Spanish was never really used.

When I was five years old, I knew about 50%; I was still learning to speak it, but comprehending I got it well.

I use Mam all the time as a way to communicate with my parents and because some words I say in Spanish don't come out as good as I do when I speak Mam.

I was told that Mam is spoken about half a million of Mayan people in the Guatemalan departments I was never told about the formation of Mam.

Yes, because people nowadays don't put importance in teaching their kids their own dialect, and it can affect them later on when they go visit their country because most people there aren't fluent in Spanish.

Yes, there are words that can't be articulated.

Yes, I arrived to Oakland because poverty and the dangerous things that were happening at the time was not getting any better

Yes, I always communicate in Mam with my family members

ANJELICA'S INTERVIEWS

Samuel (Mam)

My parents taught me.

Yes I did .

All of it, it's the only language I knew and communicated in .

Mostly all, I barely understand Spanish, let alone English .

I wasn't told anything.

No, I haven't .

Yes, I kind of am because a lot of people nowadays parents teaching the language to earlier generations, and I think that's how the more ancient Mam kind of changed because a lot of the words stopped being introduced to earlier generations, and they changed it and if we keep doing it soon this language might disappear and it's a big part of us that it's like what makes mayan people

Mayan.

Yes.

We came here for papers.

Yes, I do.

Margarita (Mam)

My mother taught me.

Yes it was.

I only used Mam as a five-year-old; that's the only language I knew, and also my family.

I still use it, but now I also use Spanish because everywhere I go, it's mostly Spanish or English, and I only now speak Mam with family members.

I wasn't told anything.

No one told me anything.

Yes because there is people who still use that language and only that language and its a nice language like its something special to know the language and if it disappears then it will no longer be there.

Yes.

I came here because that's where my dad was when he brought us from Guatemala.

Yes, I do.

Dennis (Spanish)

My family taught me.

Yes, Mam was my first language.

All of it, I lived in Guatemala, and that's the only language me and my family spoke.

I still mostly use Mam, but now, with my mom and siblings, we also speak Spanish, and I speak English too, so I use that too.

I wasn't really told anything about the history.

Yes, my grandmother told me that the Mam we use now is not the same that was used years ago.

It has changed the way it sounds and is spoken. She said that man is a formation of a man that was different, sounded different, and used by our great great great grandparents.

Yes, because it makes us who we are. It's a special part of us, and having it disappear is like a part of us is gone.

Yes many things.

We came for us to arrange papers and stay in the U.S.

Yes, I still do.

Jorge (Mam)

My parents and siblings taught me to speak it .

Yes, it was my first language.

I used it always. It was the only language I spoke.

Mostly a lot because I speak the same language at home with my kids and only not use it like at stores and work.

No, no one has ever told me any history of Mam.

No never heard any stories about the formation .

No, I am not worried about that because people in my country still mostly speak it.

Yes, a lot of it .

I came here because I heard that they have laws for you to make a case to get papers.

Yes, I still communicate with family members in Mam when contacting family in Guatemala.

Vicente (Mam)

I learned it because my parents taught me, and everyone around me spoke Mam.

Yes, it was my first language.

100%, it was the only language I used and heard.

Mostly every time except for work and going to stores .

I was never told anything about it.

No, I haven't heard any stories.

Yes I am worried because I don't want the language to get lost because my parents and other people only know that language and I think it's a beautiful thing to know that ancestral language and I want my kids, grandkids, great, -grandkids, future family members to keep the language.

Yes, there are a few things.

I came to Oakland for an asylum.

Yes, I still community with them in Mam.

Maria Matias (Mam)

I learned man because that's the language they taught me when I was born.

Yes.

I used Mam 100% when I was around 5.

About 95% because now I am learning Spanish and use it.

I wasn't told about any history.

I don't know. All I know is it came from a long line of ancestors.

Yes, I am worried because a lot of people now only speak Spanish and are teaching their kids Spanish only, too, and if it disappears, I feel like it will make us kind of disappear, too because it's like an ancestral dialect that has history and roots.

Yes, there are many things.

I came to Oakland because I heard that there was help for people for them to be able to get papers and not be deported.

Yes, I still communicate with them in Mam.

Dominga Bautista (Mam)

My parents taught me because that was their language.

Yes.

100% because that was the only language I spoke.

I still use mostly Mam except for appointments, stores, and work.

I wasn't told any history about it.

I know that it comes from ancestors, but I am not sure on the formation of it.

Yes, I am worried about it because a lot of people are not using it anymore and because it will like make us disappear kind of because it's a big part of us .

Yes there is.

I came here because I heard about people getting papers.

Yes, I only speak with them in Mam.

QUESTIONS FROM CHAPTER 8:
LINGUISTIC RESEARCH

1. How do Olimpas Gómez López and Jose Andrade Gabriel Aguilar
    highlight the significance of language in shaping cultural iden-
    tity, particularly concerning the Mayan-Mam language, and what
    strategies do they propose to preserve it within Guatemala's edu-
    cational system?

2. Considering the historical and social context outlined in the text,
    discuss the challenges and potential solutions for revitalizing in-
    digenous languages like Mayan-Mam among younger generations
    in Guatemala. How can educational institutions play a role in
    promoting linguistic and cultural diversity while respecting the
    Mayan worldview?

3. How do Nora England and Megan Simon's research shed light
    on the linguistic diversity within the Mam language, particularly
    concerning the variations in dialects?

4. Elaborate on Eliseo's explanation of the differences in Mam dia-
    lects across various regions, as described in the text.

5. How do the experiences of Mam immigrant farm workers in
    Mexico and their interactions with native speakers of Mam reflect
    the importance of language in fostering unity and a sense of be-
    longing across borders?

6. Wesley M Collins' research emphasizes the concept of centered-
    ness in the Mayan-Mam language and culture. How does Collins'
    ethnographic approach contribute to our understanding of the
    interplay between language, culture, and history within the Mam
    community?

7. Based on the interviews conducted with Guatemalan native Mam speakers in Oakland, what factors contribute to the preservation of the Mam language within the globally linked communities?

8. Reflecting on the limited historical knowledge of the Mam language revealed in the interviews, what implications does this lack of awareness have for the preservation and revitalization of Mam culture? Discuss the importance of initiatives such as Radio B'alam in Oakland and other community-driven efforts in safeguarding the linguistic and cultural heritage of the Mam people.

9

CONCLUSION

The first time I presented the manuscript of this book was to UC Davis Chicano Studies class on Central America in April 2024 hosted by Professor Yvette Flores Ortiz. Her daughter Xochi, a nurse at Highland hospital in East Oakland spoke about alcoholism amongst the Mam patients. She put me in touch with Vero, a Highland nurse originally from Guatemala. Vero described how Spanish colonial institutions and later alcohol companies would co-opt Mayan institutions, rituals and symbols. Places of sacred Mayan rituals were turned into Catholic institutions, and ceremonies would often lead to high toxic alcohol consumption. She commented on how during the civil war you could be killed for speaking an indigenous language and they carry that pain in them, leading to substance abuse. Vero pointed out that alcoholism is rampant in indigenous communities, both Mam and other native groups, with many being construction workers as their employment. Drinking beers right after work is common. Considering the work is physically difficult, consuming meth has been common. Evangelicals have used this situation to link Catholicism with alcohol abuse, as they attempt to spread their religious influence. A plethora of articles describe this problem of alcoholism in both the Mam community and other indigenous communities. Vero pointed out the parallels between the problems in Guatemala and alcoholism in native reservations here in the United States. A deeper psychological analysis is needed for the Mam community that combines the historical injustices and with such modern mental health issues. Vero's historical comments related well to the research on conditions of the indigenous communities during the civil war. But also points to modern mental health problems in the Mam community that are leading to alcoholic substance abuse. I could only hope such a history of Mam can help generate healing and mental clarity within such conditions of historical pain. In order to move forward we must overcome our past.

Thirty books, thirty academic articles, eighteen media articles, eleven academic exhibitions, and eight government documents in English and Spanish comprised the academic factual research part, and over twenty-five interviews of native Mam speakers composed the other human part of the research for this book. This book aspires to put all our findings together, historical academics with living human knowledge, to help students make sense of the history of the Mam language. Looking at their fingers and toes, the Mayans used the number twenty and math as a tool. Their math was tied to their astronomy, enhancing their science, spiritual vision, and universal understanding. The Mayans were also prolific historians, with written inscriptions documenting their own history as well as oral traditions. Uncovering the rich knowledge in language opens up many of these fields of knowledge, as language is a universal bridge of such information.

Reflecting on the history of the Mayan-Mam language, with less written history compared to their Quiché/K'iche relatives, the revitalization of Mam history is critical not only in keeping the language alive but also its history. Mam's history demonstrates an ancient tomb filled with deep wisdom and horrific pain. As new generations of young historians attempt to learn about and explain Mayan history, crossing through the linguistic, anthropological, historical, and scientific fields is key in creating a multi-disciplinary history that uncover the lost elements of the Mayan-Mam way of life.

Coupled with one's own social immersion in the community, this book could not have been possible without deep cultural insight, linguistic understanding, ethnographic work, one-on-one interviews in and on Mam, done by Lorena and Miguel. This project was a dynamic synthesis of bringing together key academic works across disciplines, with researched-centered discussions with Mam-speaking students. All of the interviewers described having knowledge of Mam that cannot be translated into Spanish or English, representing a unique body of Mayan-Mam thought. The revitalization process of Mam then contains a deeper historical importance, unearthing invisible ancient Mayan-Mam knowledge.

Historical analysis can help overcome mental paralysis. Linguistic analysis also unearths how the culture operates and views the world, as language and culture are intertwined. This research project was done in the spirit of helping Mam-speaking students access their own historical knowledge from the established academic work on the subject enhanced by ethnographic interviews with their own community. This first edition book was started only seven months ago without any funding support and was only a grassroots effort between a teacher/historian and two students. Lorena wrote in her introduction with a message to newcomers, "that come to the United States, they should never be ashamed of their cultural identity," and exerting, "we as Mayans should be able to keep the Mayan culture alive and never forget our dialect." Miguel wrote, "Educating people about the Mayan-Mam and its culture might reopen minds and keep it alive. As well as prevents its people from being ashamed of their roots, especially the never generations to come." If this book helps accomplish those goals in the slightest, then I believe the work was a success.

QUESTION FROM CHAPTER 9:

CONCLUSION

1. Why is the history of the Mam language important?

BIBLIOGRAPHY

BOOKS

Aldana y Villalobos, Gerardo *Calculating Brilliance: An Intellectual History of Mayan Astronomy at Chich'en Itza / Gerardo Aldana y Villalobos.* The University of Arizona Press, 2021.

Barry, Tom. *Roots of Rebellion: Land & Hunger in Central America (1st edition).* Edited by Tom Barry. South End Press, 1987.

Campbell, Lyle. *The Pipil Language of El Salvador / Lyle Campbell.* Berlin ; Mouton Publishers, 1985.

Carmack, Robert M., ed. *Harvest of Violence : The Maya Indians and the Guatemalan Crisis (1st edition).* Edited by Robert M. Carmack. University of Oklahoma Press, 1988.

Chang, David A. *The World and All the Things upon It : Native Hawaiian Geographies of Exploration.* University of Minnesota Press, 2016.

Chomsky, Noam. *Turning the Tide : U.S. Intervention in Central America and the Struggle for Peace.* South End Press, 1985.

Collins, Wesley M. *The Heart of the Matter: Seeking the Center in Maya-Mam Language and Culture.* SIL International, 2016.

González, Juan. *A History of Latinos in America / Juan Gonzalez* (2nd ed). Penguin Books, 2022.

Grandin, Greg. *Latin America in the Cold War*. University of Chicago Press, 2004.

---. *The Blood of Guatemala : A History of Race and Nation*. Duke University Press, 2000.

Grenoble, Lenore A., and Lindsay J. Whaley, eds. *Endangered Languages : Language Loss and Community Response*. Cambridge University Press, 1998.

Janson, Tore, et al. *A Natural History of Latin: The Story of the World's Most Successful Language* (1ˢᵗ ed). Oxford University Press, 2007.

Johansen, Bruce E. (Bruce Elliott). *Forgotten Founders : Benjamin Franklin, the Iroquois, and the Rationale for the American Revolution / by Bruce E. Johansen*. Ipswich, Mass: Gambit, 1982.

Judith L. Aissen, Nora C. (eds.) *The Mayan Language* (1ˢᵗ ed). Routledge/ Taylor & Francis, 2017.

Mann, Charles C. *1491: New Revelations of the Americas before Columbus* (1ˢᵗ ed.). Knopf, 2005.

McCreery, David *Rural Guatemala, 1760-1940*. Stanford University Press, 1994.

Menchú, Rigoberta, and Elisabeth Burgos-Debray. *I, Rigoberta Menchú : An Indian Woman in Guatemala* (Translated by Ann Wright). Verso, 1984.

Nim B'ajlom, Mateo G.R., Sandra Chigüela, and Sandra. *A Comparison of Four Mayan Languages: From México to Gutemala*. B'ajlom ii Nkotz'i'i Publications, 2010.

Peterson, Jeanette Favrot, and Kevin Terraciano, eds. *The Florentine Codex : An Encyclopedia of the Nahua World in Sixteenth-Century México*. 1st ed. University of Texas Press, 2019.

Pratt, Richard Henry. *Battlefield and Classroom : Four Decades with the American Indian, 1867-1904*. Edited and with an introduction by Robert M. Utley. Yale University Press, 1964.

Quiñones Keber, Eloise, ed. *Representing Aztec Ritual : Performance, Text, and Image in the Work of Sahagún*. University Press of Colorado, 2002.

Reeves, René. *Ladinos with Ladinos, Indians with Indians : Land, Labor, and Regional Ethnic Conflict in the Making of Guatemala*. Stanford University Press, 2006.

Samson, C. Mathews. "The Word of God and 'Our Words': The Bible and Translation in a Mam Maya Context." In *The Social Life of Scriptures*, edited by Vincent L. Wimbush, Rutgers University Press, 2020, 64–79. https://doi.org/10.36019/9780813548418-006.

Shell, Marc. *Wampum and the Origins of American Money*. University of Illinois Press, 2013.

Smith, Adam. *An Inquiry into the Nature and Causes of the Wealth of Nations*. Edited by Edwin Cannan. 3rd ed. Methuen, 1922.

Stephens, John Lloyd, and Frederick Catherwood. *Incidents of Travel in Central America, Chiapas, and Yucatan*. Rev. from the latest American ed. A. Hall, Virtue, & Co., 1854.

Tedlock, Dennis. *2000 Years of Mayan Literature*. With new translations and interpretations by the author. University of California Press, 2010. https://doi.org/10.1525/9780520944466.

Waters, Frank. *Mexico Mystique : The Coming Sixth World of Consciousness* (1st ed). Sage Books, 1975.

Webster, David L. *The Fall of the Ancient Maya: Solving the Mystery of the Maya Collapse*. Thames & Hudson, 2002.

Zinn, Howard. *A People's History of the United States, 1492- Present*. HarperCollins Publishers, 2003.

ACADEMIC ARTICLES

Acuna-Soto, Rodolfo, et al. "Megadrought and Megadeath in 16th Century Mexico." *Emerging Infectious Diseases vol. 8*, no. 4 (2002): 360-362. doi:10.3201/eid0804.010175.

Ayala, Jesús. "Oakland's Mayan Diaspora Overcomes Language Barriers and Finds Refuge in Radio B'alam." *Journal of Radio & Audio Media* vol. 30, no. 1 (2023): 139–164. https://doi.org/10.1080/19376529.2022.2133124.

Baron, Dennis. "The Babel Proclamation: Celebrating a Century of Banning Foreign Languages in America." *Illinois.edu.* Accessed 21 Jan. 2024. https://blogs.illinois.edu/view/25/653544.

Barrett, Rusty. "The Effects of K'ichean/Mamean Contact in Sipakapense." *Proceedings of the Annual Meeting of the Berkeley Linguistics Society* vol. 22, no. 1 (2014). https://doi.org/10.3765/bls.v22i1.1349.

Blume, Anna. "Maya Concepts of Zero." *Proceedings of the American Philosophical Society* vol. 155, no. 1 (2011): 51–88.

Brito Guadarama, Baltazar. "El Códice Maya de México. Códice Grolier." In *El Códice Maya de México*, edited by Instituto Nacional de Antropología e Historia, 1–14. Ciudad de México: Instituto Nacional de Antropología e Historia, 2018.

Burt, Jo-Marie. "From Heaven to Hell in Ten Days: The Genocide Trial in Guatemala." In *Guatemala, the Question of Genocide*, edited by T. W. C. Ming Hsu and Robert J. Sharer, 11-36. Routledge, 2018.

Carmack, M. Robert. Reviewed Work(s): *Piety, Power, and Politics: Religion and Nation-Formation in Guatemala, 1821-1871 by Douglass Sullivan-Gonzalez. The Annals of the American Academy of Political and Social Science* Nov. 1999, vol. 566, The Social Diffusion of Ideas and Things (Nov. 1999): 169-171.

Chomat, A.M., Solomons, N.W, and Scott, M.E. "Quantitative Methodologies Reveal a Diversity of Nutrition, Infection/Illness, and Psychosocial Stressors During Pregnancy and Lactation in Rural Mam-Mayan Mother–Infant Dyads From the Western Highlands of Guatemala." *Food and Nutrition Bulletin*, 2015. https://doi.org/10.1177/0379572115610944.

Collins, Wesley M. "The Center as Cultural and Grammatical Theme in Mam (Maya)." *Space and Culture* vol. 13, no. 1 (2010): 17–31.

Cutipa-Zorn, Gavriel. "Israel, Guatemala, and the Agricultural Roots of an Authoritarian Internationalism." *Cultural Dynamics* vol. 31, no. 4 (2019): 350–364. https://doi.org/10.1177/0921374019860941.

England, Nora. "To Tell a Tale: The Structure of Narrated Stories in Mam, a Mayan Language." *International Journal of American Linguistics* 75, no. 2 (2009): 207-231.

Gardner, Jeffrey A., and Patricia Richards. "The Spatiality of Boundary Work: Political-Administrative Borders and Maya-Mam Collective Identification." *Social Problems (Berkeley, Calif.)* vol. 64, no. 3 (2017): 439–455

Gulden, Timothy R. "Spatial and Temporal Patterns in Civil Violence: Guatemala, 1977–1986." *Politics and the Life Sciences* vol. 21, no. 1 (2002): 26–36. https://doi.org/10.1017/S0730938400005736.

Hanks, William F. "Birth of a Language: The Formation and Spread of Colonial Yucatec Maya." *Journal of Anthropological Research* vol. 68, no. 4 (2012): 1-.

Hernández Castillo, Rosalva Aída. "Cross-Border Mobility and Transnational Identities: New Border Crossings Amongst Mexican Mam People." *Journal of Latin American and Caribbean Anthropology* 17, no. 1 (2012): 65–87.

Jones, David S. "Virgin Soils Revisited." *William and Mary Quarterly* vol. 60, no. 4 (2003): 703–742. https://doi.org/10.2307/3491697.

Kaufman, Terrence. "Archaeological and Linguistic Correlations in Mayaland and Associated Areas of Meso-America." *World Archaeology* vol. 8, no. 1 (1976): 101–118. https://doi.org/10.1080/00438243.1976.9979655.

Lopez, Olimpas Gómez. *El Idioma Maya Mam y la Identidad Étnica de los Estudiantes.* Tesis presentada al Consejo Directivo de la Escuela de Formación de Profesores de Enseñanza Media de la Universidad San Carlos de Guatemala. Previo a conferirsele el grado académico de: Licenciada en Educación Bilingüe Intercultural con Énfasis en la Cultura Maya. Guatemala, septiembre 2015.

Matthew, Laura, and Sergio F. Romero. "Nahuatl and Pipil in Colonial Guatemala: A Central American Counterpoint." *Ethnohistory* 59 (2012): 765-783.

Mizuno, Takeya. "Government Suppression of the Japanese Language in World War II Assembly Camps." *Journalism & Mass Communication Quarterly* vol. 80, no. 4 (2003): 849–865.

Moseley, Christopher, ed. (2010). *Atlas of the World's Languages in Danger*. Memory of Peoples (3rd ed.). Paris: UNESCO Publishing. ISBN 978-92-3-104096-2. Retrieved 2015-04-11.

Noguez, Xavier, et al. "Códices Mayas." *Arqueología Mexicana: Códices Prehispánicos y Coloniales Tempranos – Catálogo* (in Spanish) no. 31 (August 2009): 10–23.

Parsons, Lee Allen. "The Origins Of Maya Art: Monumental Stone Sculpture Of Kaminaljuyu, Guatemala and the Southern Pacific Coast." *Studies in Pre-Columbian Art and Archaeology* no. 28 (1986): i–216. http://www.jstor.org/stable/41263466.

Pye, Clifton. "Documenting the Acquisition of Indigenous Languages." *Journal of Child Language* vol. 48, no. 3 (2021): 454–479. https://doi.org/10.1017/S0305000920000318.

Pye, Clifton, and Barbara Pfeiler. "The Acquisition of Directionals in Two Mayan Languages." *Frontiers in Psychology* vol. 10 (2019): 2442. https://doi.org/10.3389/fpsyg.2019.02442.

Sharer, Robert J., and Loa P. Traxler. "The Ancient Maya." *Journal of Latin American Anthropology* vol. 11, no. 1 (2006): 220–222. https://doi.org/10.1525/jlca.2006.11.1.220.

Spence, Jack; Dye, David R.; Worby, Paula; de Leon-Escribano, Carmen Rosa; Vickers, George; Lanchin, Mike. "Promise and Reality: Implementation of the Guatemalan Peace Accords." *Hemispheres Initiatives*. Retrieved 2006-12-06.

Vanthuyne, Karine, and Marie Christine Dugal. "Regenerating Maya-Mam Ways of Governing

Indigenous Emancipatory Politics in the Age of the Extractive Imperative." *Journal of Latin American and Caribbean Anthropology* vol. 28, no. 3 (2023): 251–260.

ACADEMIC DOCUMENTS AND EXHIBITIONS

Aguilar, Jose Andrade Gabriel. *"Pérdida de la identidad cultural maya Mam en los niños por la práctica del idioma castellano en la escuela."* Escuela de Formación de Profesores de Enseñanza Media. Universidad de San Carlos de Guatemala. Guatemala, julio de 2016.

Coffey, Sergia. "The Influence of the Culture and Ideas of the Iroquois Confederacy on European Economic Thought." *Abstract.*

Gómez López, Ely Olimpas. *"El Idioma Maya Mam y la Identidad Étnica de los estudiantes."* Tesis presentada al Consejo Directivo de la Escuela de Formación de Profesores de Enseñanza Media de la Universidad San Carlos de Guatemala. Septiembre 2015.

"Lienzo de Quauhquechollan Exhibition." *Utmesoamerica.org*, The Mesoamerica of the University of Texas. https://utmesoamerica.org/lienz o-de-quauhquechollan-exhibition. Accessed 18 Feb. 2024.

"Mam Maya." eHRAF World Cultures. Available at: https://ehrafworld-cultures.yale.edu/cultures/nw08/summary.

Stanford.edu. https://web.stanford.edu/~hakuta/www/policy/ELL/time-line.html. Accessed 15 Feb. 2024.

Stela. The British Museum. Retrieved December 29, 2023, from https://www.britishmuseum.org/collection/object/E_Am1928-Q-79.

"Mayan languages." Sam Noble Museum - The Sam Noble Museum at The University of Oklahoma Inspires Minds to Understand the World through

Collection-Based Research, Interpretation, and Education Sam Noble Museum. https://samnoblemuseum.ou.edu/collections-and-research/eth-nology/mayan-textiles/mayan-textiles-background/mayan-languages/. Accessed 31 Oct. 2014.

McCreery, David. "Debt Servitude in Rural Guatemala, 1876-1936." *The Hispanic American Historical Review*, vol. 63, no. 4, 1983, 735-. https://doi.org/10.2307/2514903.

Simon, Megan, "A Phonetic Distance Approach to Intelligibility between Mam Regional Dialects" (2019). Master Thesis. 5045.

Spence, Jack; Dye, David R.; Worby, Paula; de Leon-Escribano, Carmen Rosa; Vickers, George; Lanchin, Mike. "Promise and Reality: Implementation of the Guatemalan Peace Accords." Hemispheres Initiatives, University of Texas. August 1998.

"Authenticating the oldest book in the Americas." YaleNews. https://news.yale.edu/2017/01/18/authenticating-oldest-book-americas. Accessed 18 Jan. 2017.

MEDIA ARTICLES

Andrews, T. "A Brief History of Native American Languages in the U.S." Interpreters and Translators, Inc. February 25, 2020. https://ititranslates.com/blog/a-brief-history-of-native-american-languages-in-the-us/.

Barbeito, C. "Farmworker Charged in Officer's Heart Failure Death During Arrest." Mitú. January 3, 2024. https://wearemitu.com/wearemitu/news/guatemalan-farmworker-charged-death-police/.

Carcamo, Cindy. "Ancient Mayan Languages Are Creating Problems for Today's Immigration Courts." *Los Angeles Times*, August 9, 2016.

"Guatemala - Civil War, Human Rights, Refugees." *Encyclopedia Britannica*, n.d.

Garces, Shantal. "The Origins of the Mayan Language and How It's Survived to Today." *Babbel Magazine*, Babbel, June 12, 2023. https://www.babbel.com/en/magazine/mayan-language.

Helling, S., & Algar, S. "Charges Dropped Against Migrant Accused in the Death of Florida Deputy Who Had Heart Attack After Struggle." *New York Post*, March 2, 2024. https://nypost.com/2024/03/01/us-news/charges-dropped-against-migrant-accused-in-the-death-of-florida-deputy-who-had-heart-attack-after-struggle/.

"Language Data for Guatemala." *Translators without Borders*, February 10, 2020. https://translatorswithoutborders.org/language-data-for-guatemala.

"Language Revitalization in Oakland: A Visual Interview with Tessa Scott." *Social Science Matrix*, August 21, 2023. https://matrix.berkeley.edu/research-article/language-revitalization-in-oakland-a-visual-interview-with-tessa-scott/.

Martinez, Jose. CBS News. "Community in Oakland's Fruitvale District Works to Save Ancient Guatemalan Language." September 27, 2023

Merchan, D. "Petition Calls for Release of Guatemalan Teen Charged with Officer's Death Following Heart Attack." *ABC News*, January 10, 2024.

Middleton, Florence, "How one health center is serving Oakland's growing Mam community" The Oaklandside, Dec 12th, 2022.

Minster, Christopher. "Francisco Morazan: The Simon Bolivar of Central America." *ThoughtCo*, August 30, 2018. https://www.thoughtco.com/biography-of-francisco-morazan-2136346.

Nolan, R. "Guatemalan Child Refugees, Then and Now (disponible en español)." *NACLA*. Retrieved December 31, 2023, from https://nacla.org/news/2021/04/23/guatemalan-child-refugees-then-and-now-disponible-en-espa%C3%B1ol.

Romero, F. J. "Do You Speak Mam? Growth of Oakland's Guatemalan Community Sparks Interest in Indigenous Language." *KQED*. Retrieved December 27, 2023, from https://www.kqed.org/news/11763374/do-you-speak-Mam-growth-of-oaklands-guatemalan-community-sparks-interest-in-indigenous-language.

Devarajan, Kumari. "Ready for A Linguistic Controversy? Say 'Mmhmm.'" *NPR*, August 17, 2018. https://www.npr.org/sections/codeswitch/2018/08/17/606002607/ready-for-a-linguistic-controversy-say-mhmm.

"Maya Glyphs." *Jaguarstones.com.* https://www.jaguarstones.com/maya/glyphs.html. Translated by Content Engine LLC. "Maya-Mam Ethnic Group, on the Verge of Disappearing Due to Lack of Government Support." *C.E. Noticias Financieras*, English ed., ContentEngine LLC, a Florida limited liability company, 2022.

"The History of the Mayan Languages." *YouTube*, The Dragon Historian, https://www.youtube.com/watch?v=mBxEMGR2jNY.

"June 27, 1954: Elected Guatemalan Leader Overthrown in CIA-Backed Coup." *Zinn Education Project*, https://www.zinnedproject.org/news/tdih/jacobo-arbenz-guzman-deposed/.

GOVERNMENT DOCUMENTS

Congress, United States. 1898. *Congressional Edition.* U.S. Government Printing Office, 1–PA23. Retrieved July 20, 2017.

"The Dresden Codex." PDF. Retrieved from the Library of Congress, <www.loc.gov/item/2021667917/>.

"Guatemala - Countries - Office of the Historian." *State.gov*. Retrieved December 8, 2023, from https://history.state.gov/countries/guatemala.

U.S. Department of Justice Executive Office for Immigration Review Statistics Yearbook FY DOJ Executive Office for Immigration Review (EOIR). 2017. *Justice.gov*. https://www.justice.gov/eoir/page/file/1107056/download.

"Documentos de la Union Centroamericana" (PDF). Organization of American States – Foreign Trade Information System (in Spanish). Retrieved October 12, 2014.

"Language Revitalization in Oakland: A Visual Interview with Tessa Scott." August 21, 2023. *Social Science Matrix*. https://matrix.berkeley.edu/research-article/language-revitalization-in-oakland-a-visual-interview-with-tessa-scott/.

Press Releases Office of the High Commissioner for Human Rights Pillay Welcomes Historic Genocide Judgment in Guatemala. May 13, 2013.

The World Factbook, Central Intelligence Agency, 2023-08-29.

INDEX

A

Academia de Lenguas Mayas de Guatemala (ALMG), 69, 71
Aguilar, Jose Andrade Gabriel, 80, 81n187, 109
Aldana, Gerardo, 28
Algar, S., 1n6, 2n10
Alvarado, 39
An Intellectual History of Mayan Astronomy at Chich'en Itza, 28
Ancient Mayan languages, 73n173
Anjelica's interviews, 103
Arévalo, Juan José, 58
Armas, Carlos Castillo, 57, 59
artificial intelligence, 7
Assembly camps, 5
authoritarian internationalism, 65, 66n159
Ayala, Jesus, 76, 77n180
Ayala, Ninoska, 77

B

B'ajlom, Nim, 7, 8n30
Baron, Dennis, 5n22
Barrett, Rusty, 23n69
Barrios, Rufino, 52
Barry, Tom, 55n136
Blume, Anna, 25n75

C

Cambell, Lyle, 11, 17n51, 19n57, 22n65
Cartwright, M., 15n49
Castellano, xix, 79, 81n187
Castillo, Rosalva Aída Hernández, 42, 43n108, 52n131, 56n138, 85n195, 86n196
Chang, David, 5n20
Chichen Itzá, 27, 46
Chigüela, Sandra, 7, 8n30
Civil war, 2, 10, 50, 56, 74, 79, 111–112
Codex, 22, 28, 42, 44–46
	Dresden Codex, 45–46
	Grolier Codex, 45
	Madrid Codex, 45
Coffey, Sergia, 47
Collins, Wesley M., 3n11, 11, 44, 86n198
Colombus, Christopher, 35
colonialism, 2, 4, 10, 17, 45, 47–48, 56, 93
Cortés, Hernán, 39
COVID-19 positivity, 77
Cutipa-Zorn, Gavriel, 65, 66n159

D

Dakin, Karen, 23

Davis, Shelton H, 65
decimal system, 27
U.S. Declaration of Independence, 49
Devarajan, Kumari, 4n16
Dugal, Marie Christine, 88
Dulles, John Foster, 57, 59

E

Early Colonial Mexico, 38
Eastern Mayan Languages, 21, 23
educational establishments, 81
Elementary and Secondary
   Education Act, 5
England, Nora, 11, 41–42,
   69n167, 82, 84, 86, 109

F

Father Ximénez, 43, 48
Federal Republic of Central
   America, 50
Florentine, 41–42

G

Gardner, Jeffrey A., 83n191
Glyphs, Maya, 25n76
Goetz, Delia, 39n94, 43n110
González, Juan, 57–58
Goodell, William, 4n17
Götze, Johann Christian, 45
Grajales, Victoriano, 55
Grandin, Greg, 51, 58–59, 67
Grenoble, Lenore A., 7n27, 8n34
Guatemalan Mayan-Mam
   speakers, 8

Guatemalan National
   Revolutionary Unity (URNG), 70
Guatemalan Spanish, 79
Guatemala's civil war, 62
Gulden, Timothy R, 64
Gulden, Timothy R., 63n149,
   64n153, 65n156
Guzmán, Jacobo Arbenz, 58

H

Hank, F. William, 41n100
Hanks, William F., 40
*Harvest of Empire: A History of
   Latinos in America*, 57
Hawaiian Kanaka, 4
Helling, S., 1n6, 2n10
history of Mam as a language,
   10–11, 13
The History of the Mayan
   Languages, 16n50
Hodson, Julie, 65

I

Independent Central America,
   49, 56
indigenous peoples, 9, 48

J

Japanese-Americans, 5
Japanese language, 5
Jones, David S., 39

K

Kaufman, Terrence, 10n45,
   11n46, 30n85

K'iche (Quiché), 21–22, 39, 43, 112

L

Linguistic Research, 69, 71, 79, 109
Linguistics, 2, 79, 83, 86–87
López, Olimpas Gómez, 81, 109
Lorena's interviews, 98

M

Mam populations, 3, 43
Mann, Charles G., 10n40
Martin, Miguel Ortiz, xix
Martinez, Jose, 3n12, 67n164
Matthew, Laura, 23n70
Mayan:
    glyphs, 16, 25n76, 26
    language family, xxvii, 9, 18
    languages, 16, 18–19, 21, 29–30, 33, 35, 42, 52
    mathematics, xxv, 3, 25–26, 28
    people, 25, 75–77, 101, 103–104
Mayan-Mam Language, xxv, xxviii, 80–81, 86, 109, 112
Mayan, Yucatecan, 19
McCreery, David, 37, 55
Menchu, Menchu Rigborta, 52, 66–67
Menchú, Rigoberta, 21, 44n114, 52, 66–67
Mendez, Virgilio Aguilar, 1
Mendoza, Lorena, xv
Merchan, D., 2n7
Mexican-American war, 4

Middleton, Florence, 77
Miguel's interviews, 94
Mizuno, Takeya, 5n23
Museo Arqueológico Nacional, 45

N

Nahua, xxvii, 42n103, 55
Nahuan language, xxvii
New Testament of the Bible, 54
Nicholson, H. B., 42n104
Nolan, R., 65n155

O

Oakland:
    hills, xxv
    schools, 8, 10
Ortiz, Yvette Flores, 111

P

Pablo, Crecencio Ramirez, 76
A People's History of the United States, xxvi, 36, 37n88
Peterson, Jeanette Favrot, 42n103
Pfeiler, Barbara, 11n46, 21n64
Popol Vuh, 39n94, 40n98, 43–44, 48
Pratt, Richard Henry, 4n19
present-day Mam territory, 22
Proto-Mayan languages, 11
Proyecto Lingüístico Francisco Marroquín (PLFM), 68–69
Pye, Clifton, 8, 10n42, 11n46, 21n64, 22n67

R

Reagan, Ronald, 5

Reducción, 40–41
Richards, Patricia, 83n191
Ríos, José Efraín, 67–68
Rivera, Diego, 57
Romero, F. J., 8n32
Romero, Sergio F., 23
Roosevelt, Franklin D., 58
Roosevelt, Theodore, 5
Rural Guatemala, 37, 55

S

Sáenz, Josué, 45
Samson, Mathews C., 54n134
Shell, Marc, 3n15, 4n18
Simon, Megan, 5, 83, 109
Smith, Adam, 47
Spanish Colonialism, 2, 10, 17,
    43, 45, 47–48, 56
Spanish-speaking Mexican, 4
Spence, Jack, 75n175
Stephens, John Lloyd, 53n133

T

Tedlock, Dennis, 17, 29
Traxler, Robert J., 45n115
20th century Guatemala, 57,
    59–60

U

Ubico, Jorge, 58
Uto-Aztecan language, xxvii

V

Vanthuyne, Karine, 88

W

Waters, Frank, 39n97
Wesley M Collins' research, 109
Western decimal count system, 26
Western Mayan Languages, 20
World War I, 5
World War II, 5

Z

Zinn, Howard, xxvi, 36–37

Mira ese niño: tiene sangre india y cara española. Miralo bien: fijate que habla maya y escribe castellano. En él viven las voces que se dicen y las palabras que se escriben. No es de la tierra ni del viento. En él, la razón y el sentimiento se trenzan. No es de abajo ni de arriba. Está donde debe estar. Es como el eco que funde con nuevo nombre, el la altura del espíritu, las voces que se dicen y las voces que se callan.

Look at that child: he has indigenous blood and a Spanish face. Look at him carefully: notice that he speaks Mayan and writes Spanish. The voices that are said and the words that are written live in it. It is not from the earth or the wind. In it, reason and feeling intertwine. It is neither from below nor from above. It is where it should be. It is like the echo that blends with a new name, the height of the spirit, the voices that are spoken, and the voices that are silent.

Canek: Historia y leyenda de un héroe maya by Ermilio Abreu Gomez

a	*b*	*c*	*d*	*e*	*f*
IMIX		IK		AKBAL	KAN
g	*h*	*i*	*j*	*k*	*l*
CHICCHAN		CIMI	MANIK	LAMAT	
m	*n*	*o*	*p*	*q*	*r*
MULUC			OC		CHUEN
s	*t*	*u*	*v*	*w*	*x*
	EB		BEN		IX
y	*z*	*a'*	*b'*	*c'*	*d'*
MEN	CIB	CABAN		EZNAB	CAUAC
e'	*f'*	*g'*	*h'*	*i'*	*j'*	*k'*
			AHAU			

Made in the USA
Middletown, DE
04 May 2024

53844704R00097